MAKING THE MOST OF YOUR FREE LUNCH AT COLLEGE

BY

MORRIS SEESKIN

First Printing

2004 Morris Seeskin, all rights reserved

To Beth, Aaron, Jonathan, and Joel

PREFACE

As my step daughter, Beth, matured from a bored seventh grader, who saw no reason to plan for going to college, into a high school freshman afraid of taking courses that she believed would have too much reading, and eventually into a student at the Medill School of Journalism of Northwestern University, we had many conversations about learning, education, growing up, taking responsibility for oneself, and doing well in school.

I had similar discussions with my oldest son, Aaron, although he never had doubts about going to college. Starting in junior high school he and I started talking about where he would go to college and what he would study. After he returned from six months abroad as a foreign exchange student during his junior year, Aaron changed his focus from mathematics, physics, or engineering at Stanford or MIT to international relations at Duke, Georgetown, or ultimately Johns Hopkins.

Jonathan, my middle son, was going to be an actor, a writer, or maybe a psychologist. When he started college, he planned to major in economics at Northwestern. During his second quarter he transferred from the College of Arts and Sciences into the School of Speech to major in theater design. A year later he was back in Arts and Sciences majoring in comparative religion and thinking about becoming a rabbi. Confused, he dropped out of school for a quarter, returned, and then quit altogether. After a couple of years of work, he talked about going back to college to get his degree, but instead enrolled in some computer training classes and now does computer programming for a cutting-edge corporation.

As a child my youngest son, Joel, was the smartest kid I had ever met. Once he got to school, he decided that he didn't want to stand out among his peers. For a long time he refused to do homework and got grades that reflected his effort. He and I talked about learning and growing. He chose to ignore me and worked on doing book reports without having read the books. I tried to keep his focus on reading and developing problem solving skills. In his senior year of high school, he finally knuckled down, made the Honor Roll, and pulled up his class rank enough to get admitted to Illinois State University. He thought he wanted to be a teacher!]]\After struggling to stay in school, he switched his major and worked his way up from being on academic probation to the Dean's List. He hoped to become a professional baseball umpire, but now is in charge of transportation logistics for a corporation.

This book is an organized outgrowth of those many often disconnected conversations. I have attempted to put down on paper in a somewhat organized way what I have learned through my own experience and vicariously through others about becoming an adult in college.

At various times while in college and graduate schools I have lived in a dorm, at home, and in both on-campus and off-campus apartments. I went to school near the city in which I grew up and later halfway across the country. I nearly flunked out of college during my freshman year and later won academic honors. Along the way I got my shares of A's and B's, too many C's, two

D's and an F. I made and lost friends, sat home on Saturday nights, dated, became engaged, and married. I moved away from my religion. I took a wide variety of courses and by some standards read widely. I never stopped thinking about my own education and the educational process.

Since my college days, I have been a VISTA volunteer, been unemployed at times, been a construction worker, and now practice law in my own firm. I have found renewed meaning in my religion. I had two sons, got divorced, remarried (gaining a daughter in the process) and had another son. I became more involved in local politics and much more of an activist. I was in therapy for a while and moved on. I read more, then less, and then a lot more.

My odyssey has led me away from certainty and to a better understanding of myself. I wrote this book for my children. As each entered college I gave her or him a copy of my then current draft, hoping that it would be helpful. I hope it will be helpful for you, too.

SOME PRELIMINARY THOUGHTS

At your first glance this may seem to you to be a "HOW TO SUCCEED" book, and in one sense it is. It does contain a number of simple and not so simple hints for making your college experience more meaningful while you earn better grades.

You should not be confused, however. In fact, this is much more of a "WHO" book - who you are, who you want to be now, and who you want to become. It will not answer these questions for you, but it will deal with some practical ways that the becoming process works and how mastering the process can lead you to your own answers.

I

KEEP ON TRUCKING

You did not get admitted into college simply because you are cute. Neither were you admitted just because you are smart, talented, athletic, etc. Rather, you were admitted because of the total person you are.

The admissions officers at your college decided to accept you because you are smart and you are likely to become smarter. They believed that you would become an asset to their school. Your curiosity, intelligence, talent, maturity and integrity have been recognized by your parents, friends, and many of your teachers, even if you did not always believe them. You should be proud of what you have already accomplished, confident of your own abilities, and optimistic about your future.

If you are one of those many people who react negatively to being told what you should or should not do, please bear with me. I am not telling you what to do. Rather, I have endeavored to suggest and recommend in this book, but sometimes I want to be a little more emphatic than that. I realize that I am hardly in a position to tell you what you should or should not do. If you are honest about it, though, you probably will have to admit to yourself that you are not so sure about what you should or should not do in college. That is why you are reading this book.

In college nothing will be handed to you, on a

silver platter or otherwise. In order to succeed, do what you need to do the old fashioned way - work for it. "No pain, no gain" originally was meant to apply to physical conditioning or athletic endeavors, but it applies just as well to intellectual accomplishments.

You may not think of yourself as being particularly good looking, but you can substitute just about any other attribute you may have for "cute". There are a lot of superb high school athletes, actors, musicians, artists, writers, scientists, etc., who never make it to or through college even with their obvious talents. One of the smartest people I ever met could not deal with the pressures of college, dropped out, and the last I heard was working as a laboratory assistant.

I went to a highly competitive university and so have three of my children. The youngest enrolled at a much less selective school. If you are going to a less competitive school, this book should be just as helpful as it will be for those attending the most rigorous universities. In my original draft of this book I called each of the chapter headings a "Rule", but that designation seemed too emphatic. Rather, this book is more accurately treated as suggestions. I do not mean to imply, however, that you can take or leave these suggestions.

Although nothing at all will be handed to you in college, a lot will be made available to you. You must look for it and know what to do with it once you find it. A lot more, more than you would imagine, is just waiting for you, if only you will locate it, accept it, and use it to your advantage.

While doing research for a major political science paper in college, I discovered, in the bowels of the main library stacks, a wonderful book that was most helpful to me in crystallizing my thinking on the matter I was studying. When I checked it out, I discovered that not one student or professor in the previous thirty years had withdrawn that book from the library. Later the library was computerized and if no one else has checked out the book in the fifty plus years since I did, probably there will be no way for the next reader to know. It was as if that singular book had been hibernating undisturbed all that time, waiting to magically come alive before my eyes.

In any case, what will be important to you is not so much what you learn, how you learn it, or even from what source you learn it. Rather what will be most important is what you do with what you learn.

Several years after he had dropped out of high school one of my clients got his GED and decided to go on to college on a part-time basis. He began by enrolling in a couple of courses at the local junior college. One day while we were talking about his recent return to school, he told me that he had to leave our meeting because he was going to the "brain crusher". I thought that he would be a lot better off if he began to view both his college and the educational process as a "brain expander" or a "brain stimulator". He never did and he never completed college.

II

SCOTTY CAN'T BEAM YOU UP

No one else can do the work for you. It is truly amazing to me how many college students believe that they should be able to complete the necessary educational studies without doing much work, if any at all. You would think that after thirteen years of elementary school, middle school or junior high school, and high school that students would get the idea, but many do not. Why do you think they call it work?

Doing the minimum will get you the minimum. If you want to do well in college, learn as much as you can and then learn some more. It was not until many years after I had finished my formal education that I came to understand that learning all that I thought I could always involved learning substantially less than I was really capable of learning. Learning all that you can is an impossibility. Believing that you have learned all that you could is a dis.

What you have learned in one course or outside of class altogether can be applied and should be applied in other courses. What you learn once may later be forgotten, but it cannot be taken away from you by anyone else. Of course, what you do learn and later forget cannot be used by you in any subsequent courses This will work to your disadvantage if you are one of those people who takes great pride in forgetting everything you purportedly "learned" in class
thirty seconds after your final exam is completed. Whatever you fail to learn in the first place you can never forget.

Most American colleges seem to work on a system that promotes a "cram and forget" learning technique. My late friend Bernard Abraham, then an emeritus professor of physics at Northwestern University, in his comments on one of my early drafts thought that the problem was with students and not the colleges. My own opinion is that the common system by which college students take many unconnected courses tends to promote "cram and forget" practices among students. Those colleges with well-defined "core" programs, such as the University of Chicago, probably do a better job at encouraging systematic learning.

Paulo Freire, a renown Brazilian educator, describes this as a "banking" theory of education in which teachers make deposits into the minds of their students, who then expend those deposits from their accounts (minds). Despite this system, it is likely that the intellectual investors and not the spenders will be the leaders of tomorrow. You must choose now which you will be.

All of your important battles will be fought within you. I first learned this while trying to do intellectual battle with Paul Schilpp, one of my philosophy professors in college. I quickly forgot it and I had to learn it again years later from Dr. Ray Robertson, my therapist.

If you do not have such excellent teachers and you do have the opportunity, be sure to read <u>If You Meet The Buddha Along The Way, Kill Him</u> by Sheldon B. Kopp, who gets credit for the words if not the concept. If you do not have such an opportunity, make the opportunity and read it anyway. Kopp's "Laundry List" should be pinned to everyone's bulletin board, particularly yours, and read daily.

Learn more. Do more. Be More.

Taking responsibility for your own education and your own life generally is clearly one of the central themes of this book. Looking back on those times when I was most inclined to blame my parents, my teachers, fate, the system, bad luck, the competition, etc. for whatever was going wrong with my life, I have later seen that those were the times when I was acting the most immature.

Taking responsibility for yourself tends to indicate more than maturity; it also tends to demonstrate self-respect. Failure to take such responsibility is easier to identify as a fault in others and much more important to recognize in yourself.

After more than twenty-one years of my formal education and forty-five years in the real world, I can think of no course that I took at any level in which something of what I had previously learned elsewhere was not helpful. I am not talking about prerequisites. The educational process is cumulative. Everything you learn becomes part of the base upon which future learning in or out of school rests.

For several years the Prudential Insurance Company advertised in all the media that, "The future belongs to those who prepare for it." Malcolm X knew that Prudential was correct, but he also knew that the slogan was missing an essential word. He added the word so that it said, "The future belongs to those who prepare for it **today**." Prudential no longer uses the slogan, but recently I saw the Malcolm X version on a poster. Either one might just as well have stated, "The future will be brighter for those who educate themselves now."

The messages from the Madison Avenue advertising firm representing one of the world's largest insurance companies and from Malcolm X were essentially the same. The truth of their messages in no way depended on the identity of the messenger. That is a simple concept, but my experience is that most people accept or reject messages based on the identity of the messenger and not the content of the message. If you don't believe me, start paying closer attention to what passes for political discourse these days.

Everyone is self-educated, but such learning will proceed more effectively in an environment in which individual learners, whether we choose to call them students or teachers, work together and stimulate each other's learning. Providing such an encouraging educational climate for both teachers and students is the essence of a college/university. Do not miss reading Zen and the Art of Motorcycle Maintenance in which Robert Pirsig explains much better than I can the true essence of college as an institution to promote higher learning.

If you think of a college merely as a place, then you are well on the way to giving yourself a lesser education. If you see college as a place to reinforce your thinking and to associate with people you are likely to agree with, you are likely to give yourself no education at all. Learning will not take place in classes taught by professors who tell you what you already know. Neither will you learn by interacting only with those with whom you agree.

When I was a sophomore in college, I took a political science course that included a section on nationalism. During one of his lectures William McGovern told us that it was his experience that the things about themselves of which people seemed to be the proudest were the things over which they had the least control. It took years before the full impact of that observation struck me.

I am proud to be an American, but I had little choice in the matter. Similarly, I am proud of my Jewish heritage, but for all practical purposes my religion was established at birth. The world is full of people who are proud of being black, white, yellow or red; of having ancestors who came from Ireland, Poland, India, Mexico, Nigeria, Korea, Egypt, etc.; of being male or female; of being tall or short; and on and on. None of them had any choice in the matter. In a way it is like rolling the dice and then being proud that you threw a six.

I am not suggesting that you should abandon pride in being who you are; I know that I am not prepared to do so. It seems to me, however, that the more unquestioning pride people have in those attributes which they cannot control, the more likely they are to de-emphasize those parts of their being over which they do have control. Such action seems to me to be self-defeating.

Being an adult involves taking responsibility for those things which you can control and accepting those things you can't change.

III

TNSTAFL
THERE'S NO SUCH THING AS A FREE LUNCH
(OR IS THERE?)

Good grades must be earned; they are neither given by professors nor received by students as gifts. The same is true for poor grades. The more you know and the better you understand, the better the grades you are likely to earn. Being aware of those things that you do not know is as important, if not more important, than what you actually know. However, grades are not usually based on your knowing that you don't know.

Doing well in any course requires that you understand the professor's lectures. Even with modern recording devices, taking a course without attending all the lectures is like fighting with one hand tied behind your back. You may win, but do you really need the handicap?

Doing well also requires that you know all the assigned material and then some, that you think for yourself, that you understand others (including but not limited to the professor) and that you communicate well what you know.

More often than not, doing only what you believe will be enough to get by will mean that you will <u>not</u> get by.

If you cannot defend your position, you are more likely to be in error. If you cannot find the words to express what you mean, you probably do not have the words or more likely truly do not know what you mean.

Every once in a while even Domino's Pizza, which used to promise to deliver your order within thirty minutes or deliver it free, was late. If you tipped the delivery person anyway (because the delay probably was not his fault), then the pizza was not really without cost. If you were a cheapskate and did not tip, then your lunch may very well have been free.

The suggestions in this book, like all others, require some flexibility on your part. Strict constructionists of any variety may have some trouble with this.

The belief that a professor has cheated you with regard to a grade is generally an example of your failure to accept personal responsibility. As an attorney I am often consulted by clients who tell me that all they want is "justice" "fairness", etc. Often what they really want from me is to help them obtain just the opposite, special treatment.

On those occasions when I thought I understood something but was unable to clearly explain my understanding to someone else, invariably I later came to realize that I did not understand as well as I had originally believed or that I had misunderstood altogether.

When I first read about the Fallacy of Misplaced Concreteness in a philosophy class, I thought I understood, but when I started to write an assigned paper on this fallacy, I had great difficulty. Rather than going back to clarify my understanding, I plowed ahead with my writing. The professor recognized that I had committed the fallacy in my paper and gave me a very generous D-.

This principle of non-explanation does not apply just in the intellectual sphere. I have discovered that arguments between parents and their children, particularly adolescents, that include expressions such as "Because I say so!" and "You don't understand!" are indicative of both participants being in error. The former "explanation" is quite likely to mean "I don't really know why, but surely I don't have to answer to you." The latter "reason" is much more apt to mean "I don't really have a good reason; I just want it my way."

Dean Harold Havighurst, who was my first year contracts professor in law school, once told our class that a particular rule of law was "historic" and then added, "When lawyers say that any particular rule of law is historic, what we really mean to say is that there is no longer any good reason for it." I have learned since then that virtually every person who makes rules at one level or another (which means just about everybody, including you and me) has their own "historic" rules. In this context "rules" must be understood in the broadest sense.

One of my favorite stories concerning historic rules is about the husband who noticed that whenever his wife cooked brisket of beef, she cut two inches off one end and then stuck the severed piece in with the rest to be cooked. When he inquired as to the reason, she admitted that she did not know why she followed this strange practice, but stated that her mother had always cooked brisket of beef that way. At his next opportunity the husband asked his mother-in-law if she cut two inches off the brisket and put the severed piece into the pot with the rest before cooking it. The woman replied that she did and that she also did not know why, but that her mother had always done it that way.

When the confused husband then asked his grandmother-in-law (I'm not sure that there is such a title, but you get the point.) The reason, the crone replied, that when her children were young a brisket large enough to feed her family was a little too big for her pot. She found it both easier and cheaper to slice a couple of inches off the brisket and put the severed end into the pot with the rest rather than to buy a bigger pot.

Every professor will have her own standards for awarding particular grades. Some will grade on a curve, which may or may not be skewed. Others will establish absolute standards, which may be easier or more stringent than would have applied had a curve been used. In law school I got the highest grade in my Civil Rights Law class, but only received a B+. Where was the curve when I needed it?

It is nearly impossible to know at the start of a course exactly what kind of effort (that is **"effort"** and not minimum average score) it will take for you to earn a specific grade in that course. A graduate student at a well-known university told me that the standards used in the introductory course for which he graded papers and exams were remarkably low. He assured me that in fact the standards were probably as follows:
    A. Writes a coherent paper in an acceptable format making a direct response to

the question and demonstrating some knowledge of course materials.
    B. Demonstrates some knowledge of course materials.
    C. Gives evidence of having attended most classes and read most materials.
    D. Seems to have no real idea what this class is about.
    F. Demonstrates no idea about the course and virtually insults the professor.

This graduate student was overwhelmed by the considerable amount of non-learning, the inability to make an argument, and the failure to perceive whether or not something was relevant demonstrated by the students. This had nothing to do with the merits of the argument made. He told me that in response to a question asking that they make an argument why something was or was not true about half the students in a class in which he was assisting could make no argument at all. He also reported to me that the professor's primary concerns seemed to be keeping the students in school, not turning them off to the subject she was teaching, and avoiding bad student evaluations.

It may be that grading standards have not just become less meaningful, but rather have deteriorated altogether since I was in college. It may also be that this lone graduate student was grading papers in an atypical class for an atypical professor.

If your professor has adopted such low standards, you may be able to get high grades for sloppy work and little learning. If you act as if your professor has adopted such low standards and you are in error, however, your sloppy work and little learning will earn you a well-deserved D or F.

If, on the other hand, you adopt my working grade standards, you will never go wrong; if anything you will do better than you anticipated. I developed these standards inductively by working from grades I received back to common elements of understanding I had in the courses I took. If grade standards have deteriorated and you proceed as if they have not, then so much the better for you and your grade-point average.

A. The A student demonstrates a clear understanding of the lectures and assigned materials with evidence of independent (creative) thinking and consideration of relevant additional (unassigned) materials.

In courses with multiple choice exams and in many introductory courses it may be sufficient to demonstrate a clear understanding of all of the lectures and assigned materials. But even in those situations demonstrating independent thinking and knowledge of relevant additional (unassigned) materials can only help you get your A.

B. The B student demonstrates a good understanding of the lectures and assigned materials but does not give evidence of independent (creative) thinking and consideration of relevant additional (unassigned) materials. In less competitive settings a good understanding may be enough to get you an A, but don't count on it.

C. The C student demonstrates a basic

understanding of the core course, but has missed some elements.

D. The D student demonstrates some understanding of the core course, but does not grasp some important concepts.

F. The F student missed the main thrust of the course.

In recent years the claim that "There is no such thing as a free lunch" has become wide spread, particularly in conservative political circles. The problem with saying "TNSTAFL" is that it is true only in the short run. The longer your time frame of reference, the more true it is that not only is there such a thing as a free lunch, but that virtually all lunches are free.

If you are convinced that there is no such thing as a free lunch, think again. You are who you are because of those who came before you and it didn't cost you anything for their gifts. You received many free meals from your parents and probably your grand-parents, to say nothing of the knowledge, understanding, and values for which they didn't charge you.

Thomas Edison invented the light bulb for you and didn't send a bill. William Shakespeare made your life richer and didn't even know you. An unknown Muslim invented the zero for your benefit. Somebody invented the wheel and the lever to make your work easier. An unknown prehistoric African woman, dubbed "Eve" passed on to you and every other <u>homo sapiens</u> the genetic code that makes you human. You owe them a remarkable debt that you never have to repay.

23

Tell Copernicus, Newton, and Darwin that there is no such thing as a free lunch. Tell Abraham, Moses, Christ, Mohammed, Confucius, and the Buddha that you owe them nothing. Next time you think about it, tell Christopher Wren that you don't need his talent. Tell Einstein and Freud that their insights are worthless to you. Think about how much duller your life would be if Mozart, Chagall, and Louis Armstrong had never been.

Some politicians are quick to claim that there is no such thing as a free lunch. In the short run, they probably are right. Everything has a cost. Too often, though, like most of us, they fail to take the longer view. The truth is that you need to be able to take both views at appropriate times. When you think you will get something for nothing, then remember **TNSTAFL**, but when you begin to focus on yourself and what you alone can accomplish, then step back and thank Euclid, John Locke, Ludvig von Beethoven, John Keats, W. E. B. DuBois, Pablo Picasso, or anybody else to whom you are indebted.

IV

WHAT IS A NICE BOY LIKE YOU DOING IN A PLACE LIKE THIS?

During the first two years that my oldest son, Aaron, was in elementary school I would attend periodic conferences with his teachers. After an initial exchange of the usual pleasantries, their message to me was always, and almost word for word, the same: "Aaron is such a bright young boy. He follows directions and is well behaved. Aaron is such a pleasure to have in my class. I really wish I had more children like Aaron in my class. You should be very proud of him."

Like most people I enjoy being flattered, at least some of the time, but I have learned that if I am not careful flattery often gets in the way of my obtaining a good understanding and appreciation of the truth.

Of course I was proud of Aaron. When he was in second grade, he started at a new school. I went to my first conference with his new teachers expecting to hear from them more of the nice but not very informative pap. I was in for quite a surprise when I met with Candas Sullivan and Fay Pais for the first time. After we introduced ourselves, sat down and exchanged a few comments to break the ice, they brought me up short by saying, "Aaron has a very strong curiosity to learn about everything and the challenge to us will be to insure that he does not lose that curiosity."

The "us" clearly referred not just to the two

teachers with whom I was talking, but also to Aaron's parents, to the school staff and administration, and to Aaron himself. These two insightful ladies were teachers in the truest sense of the word. More than thirty-five years later, while Aaron is finishing his Ph.D., the challenge is still the same for us, to make sure that Aaron does not lose his curiosity. What has changed is that more and more it has become Aaron's challenge and not so much "our" challenge.

In college there still will be a challenge to your professors, administrators, staff and parents to help maintain your curiosity, but you would do well to assume that they will not live up to it. The challenge to you in college and after will be to see that you do not lose your own curiosity. Your success in college and in life after college will be measured by your ability to meet this challenge.

If you succeed in maintaining your interest in your total college experience, the suggestions in this book will become the natural way of doing things. A healthy skepticism will help you reach your goals, but pessimism and cynicism will bar your way to success.

V

LEARNING VARIES IN PROPORTION TO THE SQUARE OF THE TIME SPENT STUDYING

The above equation is not exact because I created the statement out of whole cloth to make a point and not to state a mathematical truth. So what? (Not only is it not exact, but I don't know if it is even close.) Forget that you ever read between the parentheses and you will be much better off. In any case there are functional limits because you can only study so long without a break.

It is not just that you will learn more when you study more; you will learn **substantially** more when you study more. The time you spend studying without interruptions or distractions is worth more. By my formula one full uninterrupted hour of study is four times as effective as four fifteen minute segments. Whether or not it is actually four times as effective, I assure you that it really is more effective. Cramming for an exam at the end of the term is always worth less, but it is not worthless.

Good notes will help; poor notes will confuse. Most new college students do not know the difference between good notes and bad notes. If you wait until just before exams to review your notes, you are likely not to learn if they are good or bad until after your grades arrive. Reviewing your notes shortly after class and from time to time thereafter is the best way to determine if your notes are helpful (good) or confusing (bad).

Well researched, intelligently organized, carefully written, and properly edited papers tend to be well done. Papers done in a hurry at the last minute due to procrastination tend to be deficient. Some excellent writers may be able to throw together "A" papers, but even they would have done better with better time management.

Enrolling in a good speed reading course can help you learn how to read more material in less time with better comprehension.

What you have already learned must be reconsidered periodically, but need not be totally learned again. Everything that you have already learned should be reconsidered regularly in light of new information and ideas. Knowledge is not carved in granite, and even granite changes with the passage of enough time. Much of what you believe that you "know" today you will discard as incorrect tomorrow. That is the nature of learning.

A while back my brother, Kenneth Seeskin, a college professor, was named to an academic chair in recognition of his outstanding teaching. At his induction he spoke of another professor who had greatly impacted his work. He told those gathered that he had delivered a paper at a philosophical conference. When he was done, the next speaker rose, told those present that everything my brother had said was "asinine", and spent his allotted time ripping Ken's position.

After the day's events, Ken returned to his

hotel. He quickly decided that either his speech was "asinine" and he would have to rethink, revise, and retool his entire position, or the other speaker had been wrong, in which case Ken wanted a public apology. Ken invited his debunker to dinner and the two talked well into the early morning. When they were through, Ken knew that he had a lot of rethinking to do. Few knew until many years later why Ken had made such an abrupt and significant change in his philosophical approach.

Quick now, what is a normal human temperature as measured by an oral thermometer? The answer as we all know is 98.6 degrees Fahrenheit. At least that has been the answer for many generations. Recent studies show, however, that "normal" can range from 98 degrees to 100 degrees depending upon the time of day. It turns out that 98.6 degrees Fahrenheit is nothing more than a mathematical conversion from the Centigrade measurements made years ago in Germany with less accurate thermometers than we have today.

Happy people learn more; tired people learn less. You may believe that those who earned good grades are happy because they did well. More likely it was the other way around.

When I was in high school, I believed that I could study more effectively while I listened with one ear to a sporting event playing quietly on the radio. When Beth was in high school, she thought that she was able to study better while the latest rock music blared first from her radio in the background and later from cassette tapes that her "Walkman" piped directly into her ears. Joel, listens to CDs, MP3, etc.

29

Of course we were all wrong. In college I eventually learned to study during the day in the quiet of my room, only later finding the library. Beth learned much quicker than I in high school that she studied better in the enforced silence of the local library. Joel is a real night person. He started studying late at night and continued into the early morning. He said that both the dorm and his fraternity house were a lot quieter and more conducive to studying at 3:00 a.m. than they were at 10:00 p.m.

When Beth got to college, she stopped studying in the library, not wanting to miss the action in her dorm. (She denied that this was the reason she preferred studying there.) It took her a while, but eventually she remembered what she had forgotten about quiet studying.

If you do not believe that all such external stimuli distract from your ability to concentrate on your studies rather than enhance it, talk to any mother who has delivered her baby using prepared childbirth (such as Lamaze) techniques, which use intentionally created visual, tactile, aural, and mental stimuli to decrease the mother's conscious awareness of her very real labor pains. Also, if your dentist offers you music through earphones while working on your teeth, ask her why.

Recently I saw a television program about testing the driving skills of distracted drivers. In a controlled setting subjects were asked at different times to talk on cell phones, read, take notes, sort CDs, put on makeup, and count backward from 1,000 by sevens all while driving. Without exception the distracted drivers drove poorly. They failed to stay in their lanes, didn't stop in time to avoid hazards, collided with mock vehicles, hit pretend pedestrians and animals, and damaged their cars.

What is there that makes you think that distractions negatively impact on drivers but that similar distractions will enable you to study better?

VI

SOAP OPERAS ARE EPHEMERAL THINGS

There are only twenty-four hours in a day. (For all the literalists among you I do know that every few years the astronomers add a leap second to one day. We are dealing with concept here and not scientific exactitude.)

The time you spend doing things which do not count will not be available to you to spend on those things which do count. If you expect to find out what counts for you printed in this book, you are likely to be out of luck. I have written about the process of your determining what counts for you and not about what you determine.

The time you waste can never be recaptured; the time you spend well is always an investment in you. You have available all of the time you will ever need, but if you waste enough of it and procrastinate long enough, you will not. Several judges I know display signs that read, "Procrastination on your part does not constitute an emergency on my part."

In his campaign for the presidency then Governor Bill Clinton talked about investing rather than spending. By and large the first President Bush and the Republicans tended to belittle this distinction. Whatever your politics, I assure you that fully grasping the difference between spending and investing will pay off for you. (I first wrote about the difference between wasting time and investing time in 1985, when I started on my first draft of this book for Beth.

President Clinton didn't consult me on this, but then I'm not just following his lead.) By the way, if you are a Republican, be sure to consider the difference between the message and the messenger. See Chapter II.

OK, so you just can't get past President Clinton. Look at it a little differently. Your parents are investing in your future by paying for part or all of your education. For that matter, so are you. You may have taken out loans so that you could invest the proceeds in yourself. Why, then, should government at any level, treat money spent on education as an expense rather than an investment? In another context why is it an investment for a family to buy a home or for a business to buy a site at which it can conduct its business, but an expense for a government body to purchase a site from which to render its services?

Unless you are still living at home and desire to keep on arguing with your parents about whether or not you are wasting your time, in college you must answer to yourself about how you will effectively manage your time. Hardly anyone I have met, parent or child, will actually agree that they desire to keep on arguing, but the actions of many arguers speak louder than their words.

Many college students seem to find it quite difficult to make this adjustment and they continue acting as if the power struggle with their parents must continue, even in the immediate absence of their parents. Fortunately most eventually drop this charade.

There are no absolutes in determining what

counts for any one individual. Watching television soap operas may be time well spent for future television producers and theater critics. In moderation it may also be important relaxation time for others. Not studying enough for an exam in order to watch "General Hospital" is a waste. Attending basketball and football games may be, but it need not necessarily be, an absolute waste of time for engineering and pre-med students but essential field work for future athletic coaches, sports writers, and sociologists. Spending hours talking about football rankings, hair styles, hunks, babes, and who will run for President in the next election, when you don't really understand what is going on in your Organic Chemistry class rarely makes sense.

In college I often found that several hands of bridge were just the diversion I needed to help me get out of a stuck place. Bridge "rats", who played on right through their classes and study time could hardly say the same.

Determining what it is that actually counts for you can be done only by you. No one else can do it for you. Making the important decision (or more accurately, the important decisions) about what counts for you is a never-ending process which requires honesty, integrity, insight and intelligence - just the attributes you have - if only you will use them to your own advantage.

If you regularly find that you run short of time for doing those things that you decide count for you, keep a detailed diary of your activities for at least a week. The time that you are not using to your best advantage will become obvious and probably surprise you. Be sure that you include in your diary all of the time you spend just waiting for telephone calls, classes to begin, people to arrive, etc. Do not forget all the time you spend fooling around, chatting, daydreaming, gossiping, etc.

I have heard it suggested many times that, "the length of time that it takes to complete any task will tend to fill the time available." I have discovered that there is a lesser known "college student exception" to this general rule, namely: The length of time that it will take a college student to properly complete any class assignment will shorten or lengthen so as to not quite match the amount of time available.

I do not mean to suggest that all of the time you so spend is wasted, but I do urge you to consider whether you think that it is best for you to spend as much time as you now do on the things you choose to do. I do not have the answer for you, but you do.

Once you get into the habit of critically examining how you invest or waste your time, you will probably be able to get in an extra hour of studying every day just by constructively utilizing what would otherwise be wasted waiting time. Such time is a bonus just waiting to be claimed.

Recently I finished reading an interesting, but not too heavy, book that I carried around with me and read a few pages or a chapter at a time while I waited at rapid transit stations, stood in elevators, sat in courtrooms waiting for judges, ignored television commercials, etc. At home I always keep available for reading a "bathroom book".

The benefits to be earned from investing as little as five minutes immediately after each of your classes reviewing your just completed notes is substantial. Toss in five minutes more just before each of those classes reviewing notes from the day before and you will be adding about two and a half hours a week of the easiest and most effective studying you will ever do.

This notion is consistent with the equation in Chapter V because you will not just be adding two isolated five minute segments. Instead, by my formula you will be converting a class session of say fifty minutes into a class-study session of a full hour, resulting in a 44% increase in learning.

$$([50+10] \times [50+10]) / 50 \times 50 = 3,600 / 2,500 = 1.44$$

On the other hand merely adding two disconnected five minute study segments will only increase learning by 2%.

$$50 \times 50 + 2 \times [5 \times 5] / 50 \times 50 = 2,550 / 2,500 = 1.02$$

Stay with the concept and forget the mathematics.

VII

BAD PROFESSORS ARE A NUISANCE

You alone are responsible for your education. If a class is a bummer, you always have the opportunity to make it interesting. When I first wrote this, I came very close to stating that you have the obligation to make it interesting. That may be a bit strong, but you do owe it to yourself to get the most out of every class you take.

If a professor is boring, nothing and nobody is stopping you from learning elsewhere what you need to know. This concept was brought home to me by Paul Schilpp. He told our philosophy class, "If you can't get an education from me, get one in spite of me." Most professors will not tell you that, but it is still good advice. The professor does not have to know what you are doing.

Have you noticed how "boring" teachers seem to gravitate to certain subjects, such as plane geometry, but not algebra? I have had my share, but I suspect that such boredom has much more to do with students than it does with teachers.

Actually, I did not think that my plane geometry teacher at Proviso West High School in Hillside, Illinois was boring; I thought that he was loony. It wasn't until several years after I graduated from high school that I realized that Seth Boyd was odd in that, unlike most of my other teachers, he taught no "subject" but rather taught his students to engage in clear thinking. He refused to permit me or my classmates to slide by with anything less.

If a text is not clear, you always can reread it or read something else. If you do not feel well, make yourself feel better. If you are unable to make yourself feel better, act as if you are feeling better anyway. The result may amaze you.

Excuses and reasons for not doing well are never included on your transcript. Of what use would a transcript be that read something like:
> English 101 - B, but he missed two days due to the flu and handed in a paper that was of lower quality than he was capable of doing because he missed study time due to a big party weekend. All things considered, he might have earned an A or at least an A-, if he had worked harder and avoided the flu."

All things considered, you would be better off just taking your B and forgetting the rest.

When faced with the inevitable, humans adjust. I have my wife and law partner, Eileen Fein, to thank for this bit of wisdom. We often pass it along to our clients. Remembering it can be very comforting when you are faced with, "What will my parents do when they find out about ...," "What will my boyfriend say when I tell him ...," "If she ..., I'll just ...," and the like.

See Chapter XIX, which deals with soldiering.

Among the more feeble excuses for not doing the assigned work, not doing the work well, not completing the work on time, or not understanding either the assigned materials or the instructions (not understanding itself often being nothing more than an excuse) that I have given myself or heard given by others are the following:

1. **I don't like the professor.** Where is it written that you must be assigned to a professor that you like or that you cannot learn from a professor you dislike?

Shortly after her graduation from high school I asked Beth to identify the best teacher she had studied with in high school. She named two, one of whom she had not liked. In fact, she had tried unsuccessfully several times to drop his class. When I asked her why she chose him, Beth said that she did not like him, but that she had learned a lot from him.

2. **The professor is a jerk.** There are jerks in every profession. Why should college professors be any different? Who told you that you cannot learn what you need to know from a jerk? Notwithstanding, there is a tendency to label far too many excellent teachers as jerks. If "jerk" is my word and not yours, then feel free to insert the term of your choice.

I have learned that "I can't" usually does not mean "I am unable" in the sense of not being not being strong enough, not being smart enough, not having the capability, or not having sufficient information. Rather, it is more likely to mean that I choose not to. By substituting "I won't" for "I can't" I often discover that in fact I can if only I will make the decision and effort to do so.

3. **I can't understand the material**. If this is true, and it seldom is, then you do not belong in the course and possibly not in the school. Do not expect the professor to bring the class down to your level. What will you learn from materials that are not at least a little bit over your head? When you say "I can't understand the material" you probably mean you won't understand it.

I find playing bridge with partners and opponents who are much poorer or much better players than I am to be frustrating. I much prefer bridge with players who play at a level a little higher than I do.

4. **The professor did not make himself clear**. You may very well be correct, but you will always be better off assuming that he was perfectly clear and that you were not paying sufficiently careful attention. Either way, the problem of your not understanding is easily resolved - ask the professor for a

clarification.

I am at a loss to understand why it is that so many students from primary grades through graduate school will not ask a teacher for a clarification. If your professor is not available, talk to one of her teaching assistants. If all else fails, see if one of your classmates can help you. Do you really expect the professor to be sympathetic when you tell her that she was unclear? Don't you believe that she is likely to be more helpful when you tell her that you didn't fully understand?

    5. **This class is irrelevant**. The subject of a course may be, but almost never is, irrelevant, but expanding your personal data base and improving your intellectual skills and processes always is most relevant.

A professor I know claims that he actually believes less than half of what he says in his lectures. (I have purposely not named him, but I know him well and I am inclined to believe that his estimate is probably a bit too high.) He states that most of what he says is designed to get his students to think for themselves about the subject matter under consideration. Obviously, students who merely parrot back on the final exam what he says in class are in for quite an unpleasant surprise.

I am an attorney engaged in a general civil practice. I represent buyers and sellers of real estate, draft wills,

interpret contracts, try cases and deal with all kinds of people. Among the college courses I took as an undergraduate that I have found relevant to some aspect of my practice are:
        Spanish
        Psychology
        Sociology
        American Business History
        General Semantics
        Literature
        Logic
        American Government and Politics
        Extemporaneous Speaking
        Ethics
        Anthropology
        Intellectual History of the American Negro
        Physical Geography (map reading, meteorology, land forms, etc.)
        Law and Politics
        Calculus[1]
        Micro-Economics
        Macro-Economics
        Philosophy
        Water Safety Instructor Training (P.E.)

Among the courses I never took in college and wish I had taken because they would

---

[1] I took calculus in college and could have used it often in my practice, but unfortunately I did poorly in the course and did not learn well enough so that I could use later what I had learned.

have proven helpful to me are:
    Statistics
    More Spanish
    Automobile Mechanics (I really missed this in high school, but I had to include it in my list.)
    More Psychology
    Creative Writing
    Accounting
    Anatomy
    History of Architecture
    Physiology
    Chemistry
    Physics
    Art Appreciation
    Music Appreciation
    Comparative Religion
    Biology
    Computer Programming
    Acting
    Engineering Graphics (Mechanical Drawing)

I have spent three full years in law school and thirty-five years in practice learning how to think like a lawyer and how to find answers to ever-changing questions. Learning the "black letter" law is always the easiest part. Education is a life-long process; It is not an end. You never get an education.

The best thing I have ever read dealing with the problem of anticipating the relevancy of college and courses of study to later life was "Remarks Concerning Savages of North America" written in 1784 by Benjamin Franklin. Franklin wrote:
    At the treaty of Lancaster, in

Pennsylvania, anno 1774, between the Government of Virginia and the Six Nations, the commissioners from Virginia acquainted the Indians by a speech, that there was at Williamsburg a college with a fund for educating Indian youth; and that if the chiefs of the Six Nations would send down half a dozen of their sons to that college, the government would take care that they be well provided for, and instructed in all the learning of the white people.

The Indians' spokesman replied: We know that you highly esteem the kind of learning taught in those colleges, and that the maintenance of our young men, while with you, would be very expensive to you. We are convinced, therefore, that you mean to do us good by your proposal and we thank you heartily.

But you, who are wise, must know that different nations have different conceptions of things; and you will not therefore take it amiss, if our ideas of this kind of education happen not to be the same as yours. We have some experience of it; several of our young people were formerly brought up at the colleges of the northern provinces; they were instructed in all your sciences; but when they came back to us, they were bad runners, ignorant of every means of living in the woods, unable to bear either cold or hunger, knew neither how to build a cabin, take a deer, nor kill an enemy, spoke our language imperfectly, were therefore neither fit for hunters, warriors, nor counsellors; they were totally good for nothing.

We are however not the less obligated by your kind offer, though we decline accepting it, and to show our grateful sense of it, if the gentlemen of Virginia will send us a dozen of their sons, we will take care of their education, instruct them in all we know, and make men of them.

You might also consider that much of what you learn will not be relevant because, as Henry Adams pointed out in his autobiography, teachers tend to teach students to solve the problems of the teachers' generation. As a senior in high school I took a course in contemporary American history. The teacher spent weeks trying to get his students to think about whether on balance Franklin D. Roosevelt, who died before I was three years old, had been good for the country. We, his students, were starting to think about whether or not American "advisors" belonged in Viet Nam.

6. **This course is a waste of time.** No class can ever waste your time, but you can. Just because you fail to see the immediate importance in your life of some particular course or assignment, it does not follow that that course or assignment does not merit your time and attention.

As an undergraduate I was required to take a year of a laboratory science. I chose Introduction to Physical Geography. Several of my friends berated my choice claiming that "Phys G" was a waste of time. Chemistry, physics, biology, or even astronomy, they said, would be much more beneficial. I haven't kept a score card, and I do wish I had taken all those sciences. However, when I took the Law School Aptitude Test, the general knowledge section contained six science questions and all of them dealt with physical geography.

7. **The professor thinks that this is my only class - there is too much work.** I have met many professors who believed that theirs was the most important class, but even they were aware of normal undergraduate course loads. Usually, this excuse is merely a rationalization for sloughing off by a student who would have preferred a professor who assigned less work.

Based on the concept that the length of

time that it will take to complete any task will tend to expand or contract to fill the available time, those who make this complaint are likely to make it no matter how much or how little work the professor assigns.

On Jonathan's first day in college his macro-economics professor assigned fifty-seven pages of text for the next class. Jonathan's first reaction was mild panic, but as he put it, "Then I said to myself 'I'm in college.'" He finished the assignment that evening along with assignments in Spanish and calculus.

A corollary of this excuse is, "I didn't do well in (Class A) because I worked so hard in (Class B). Aside from the fact that a person making this excuse probably didn't work "so hard" in (Class B), almost never does doing well require that you choose between courses.

8. **I attend all the lectures so I don't have to do all the reading (or vice versa).** The professor teaches the course and has probably taught it before, sets the course requirements and grades your work. No matter what you may believe, you are always a neophyte in this course. When the professor holds all the trumps, how much are you willing to bet that you can outguess her? Does it make a difference that the professor is not required to match your bet and can neither win nor lose?

In high school teachers tend to restate

the text to their students. This is done on the theory that information inputted both aurally and visually is more likely to be retained. In college lectures and readings are more like two roads starting and finishing at the same termini, but taking somewhat different routes.

9. **There is more to college than just classes**. Of course, this is true. But it is just as true that there is very little, if anything, to college without classes. See Chapter XX. I have yet to meet a student or former student who stayed in on Saturday night because "there is more to college than just going to parties."

You probably have your own favorite excuses and in all likelihood they will not hold up any better than mine have.

At a party I met a professor who claimed that he was willing to act favorably upon any request for an extension of time to complete an assignment or take an exam, if the student offered an excuse, any excuse, but only if he had never heard that particular excuse before. He claimed that while he was essentially inclined to disbelieve all excuses, the least he could do was to reward creativity. See Chapter XXI.

He said (I cannot vouch for the truth of what he said, but it makes an interesting story.) that some years ago he refused to accept one woman's excuse that she was late handing in an assignment because she had undergone an abortion. He claimed to have heard that excuse before. On the other hand, he added, he accepted the excuse of another woman in the same class who told him that she hadn't turned in her assignment on time because she had to perform the abortion on the first woman. He did not indicate what he thought about abortion. (The point of this story has nothing to do with being pro-choice or pro-life. It does have to do with excuses.)

When you are having problems with a course, and at one time or another every student does, keeping your focus on yourself instead of on the class, the text or the professor will go a long way toward helping you avoid making excuses of any kind. Minimally you will not have to waste more time worrying about whether or not you have a good excuse. You always can improve a bad situation by improving the one element of education that only you control - you.

VIII

IT'S NOT WHO YOU KNOW THAT COUNTS, IT'S WHAT YOU KNOW

Luck tends to even out in the long run. When I first wrote this, I was thinking in the abstract. Later I read Bruce Catton's Gettysburg: The Final Fury and was taken by how different the result of that momentous battle and the entire Civil War might have been but for apparently fortuitous events. Given the circumstances, though, it is still most difficult for me to see how the result could have been substantially different. In Bring the Jubilee Ward Moore speculates on what life in the USA, which in his book excluded the Confederate States and many post Civil War states, would have been like if Pickett's charge had succeeded. It is interesting reading, but it is science fiction and not fact.

You only know those people who you know. Who you know can be important, but you have much more control over what you know. On the other hand, you do have a lot of control over who you get to know or more importantly who gets to know you.

Performance now will pay you dividends later as well as now. There is a big difference between taking a chance and investing.

If you do not understand what this has to do with succeeding in college, then you do

50

not really understand the difference between gambling and investing. Attending lectures and reading assigned materials is an investment in yourself. Skipping lectures and doing the reading or vice versa is gambling on what the minimum is that you will have to do to get by in a course.

Do not kid yourself, your grades really are important, but there is a lot more to doing well in college than just getting good grades. Grades tend to vary directly with performance.

Good performance and poor grades seldom go together. For that matter, grades seldom indicate a level of performance below that which you in fact earned. Poor performance and good grades never go together. You can't luck out. Even if you can luck out, you won't.

I took a course in extemporaneous speaking and after earning A's throughout, including the final exam, received a B for a final grade. When I discussed the matter with the professor, I learned that he did not want to give the only A in this small class to someone who was not a speech major. For every time that such a thing really happens there are probably hundreds when students believe that it happened but it did not.

In my sophomore year in high school I really did luck out in my Latin class and got a grade that was significantly higher than the one I knew I deserved. By sheer

51

accident in the hour before the final exam I studied from a practice test in a study guide I had purchased because it was the only one at my local bookstore. Much to my amazement, just an hour later I discovered that my teacher had copied the final exam verbatim from the particular practice test I had just reviewed. During the next ten years I was unable to duplicate this feat. What do you think the chances are of something similar happening to you? See Chapter III.

Mathematicians and bookies understand that in the long run luck evens out. Actually, I am not all that sure about mathematicians. Sydney J. Harris, journalist and avid bridge player, pointed out that often skilled mathematicians seem to forget what they know about odds, when they sit down at the card table. Bookies never forget the odds. Bookies also know that point spreads and pari-mutuel betting have little to do with odds.

If the odds are against you, the longer you gamble or the more you bet, the more likely you are to lose.

Casino owners understand this. They provide gamblers with free drinks, free food, and entertainment. High rollers (big betters, a/k/a whales) may also get free hotel rooms, travel, and more. The owners know that the longer they keep gamblers at the tables, the more likely that the house will grind them down. It is also the reason why casinos like big winners, who act as an encouragement to others to keep playing, hoping for the big score. If you do not understand, imagine a contest in which you and I flip silver dollars. If we match (both show heads or both show tails), then you lose and pay me a dollar. If we do not match, however, then I lose and pay you ninety cents. Do you have any doubt about who will win in the long run?

It may seem to you that purchasing two raffle tickets will double your chance of winning, but that really is not so. It only doubles your chance of winning the prize offered. If you bought all the tickets being sold, you would be guaranteed to win the prize, but you also would likely be guaranteed that the prize would be worth less than the amount you paid for all the tickets. The only exception occurs when the ticket money amounts to less than the value of the prize, such as some exotic race track bets in which prize money is carried over from previous days, when there was no winner.
Investing tends to work the opposite way. The more you invest and the more often you invest, the more likely it is that you will earn a return on your investment and the larger that return is likely to be. Most of the investment guides I have read emphasize the substantial benefits to be gained by making regular periodic investments.

The single most important thing to remember about grades is that it is you and not the professor who determines the best grade that you can earn. My

53

experience is that only those who want A's and are willing to work for then actually get them. Those who will be satisfied with B's are seldom pleasantly surprised. Those students willing to receive C's, usually make the most of their opportunity to earn them.

Do not kid yourself with self-serving rhetoric; look inside yourself instead of listening to your own words in order to determine what grades you really want to receive. If you are not willing to do the necessary work to obtain a particular grade, then you do not really want that grade and you will happily accept less.

During her first two years in college Beth got B's and C's, while telling her mother and me that she could get A's but that there was more to college than grades. The only people who got A's, she reported, had absolutely no social life and were not involved in any extracurricular activities. She said she wanted more out of her college experience. In her second two years, though, Beth's grades improved to A's and B's while she was more active in extracurricular activities and had an even better social life. What really changed were her goals and expectations of herself.

IX

LISTEN UP

Interesting men and women, exciting courses, important activities, and challenging ideas will be all around you. Not learning from them will stunt your growth. If you are interested, you will be more interesting to others; if you are more interesting to others, they will be more interested in you.

Keep good records of everything you do. Sometimes I vaguely remember something from some course of years ago but cannot lay my hands on the information because of inadequate records. On the other hand, at times Beth simply assumed that I would know where to find answers to her questions and resource materials for her papers in my own library. Often she was correct.

Make copies of everything, particularly papers you hand in. Even professors (maybe even, particularly professors) sometimes lose things. I have heard stories about Ph.D. candidates who were set back years because their one and only dissertation copy was lost, stolen or destroyed. In this context if you do your own work on a computer, be sure to back up you work regularly. Back up your back up.

Always pay careful attention to details. Challenge your own assumptions and beliefs. A healthy skepticism never retarded anyone's intellectual development.

Be open to new ideas. If you are not willing to do this, you would do well to save your time and money by dropping out of college immediately. By dropping out quickly you can open up a place for someone else who will benefit from college.

Pay attention to yourself. You cannot make anybody else happy; no one else can make you feel badly. Taking responsibility for yourself is an integral part of being an adult. The late Sydney J. Harris understood this when he wrote in one of his newspaper columns:
> We use phrases like "He makes me mad" and "She makes me sick" in order to disclaim the responsibility for our emotional responses. A food can make you sick whether you want it to or not, but another person cannot contaminate you unless you permit it.

Accept constructive criticism and use it to your own advantage. This is called learning. Learning to accept constructive criticism without hearing it as a personal attack is both difficult and essential to your educational and personal growth.

When Beth was a high school freshman, invariably she heard my suggestions and comments on her work as being rejections of her or at least of her work. Over the next two years she began to hear my constructive criticism as caring offers of help rather than personal attacks, and she learned how to use my help to her advantage. By her senior year she actively sought out my input. It was no accident that Beth raised her cumulative grade point average and class rank each and every semester.

Challenge your own assumptions, beliefs, opinions, and thoughts. The more fundamental and ingrained they are, the more they need to be challenged and tested. Your intellectual growth does not have to be a painful experience involving loss of face when you change your mind. More often than not it will be a freeing experience involving a quiet personal reassessment of your thinking rather than a loud public admission of some previous error.

I am aware that this advice would be rejected by politicians, who seem to believe that changing one's mind is a "flip-flop" and a sign of uncertainty rather than honest growth. Religious fundamentalists of any persuasion will also scorn this advice, at least in some areas. You can't please all of the people all of the time.

In the middle of an introductory class in ethics a student pointed out an apparent inconsistency between something Professor Schilpp had just said and something he had said in a previous lecture. After several minutes of silent and obviously intense reflection, Schilpp said, "You know, I have been teaching it that way for years, and you are right. There is an inconsistency." He then proceeded to rethink aloud the matter under consideration. Not only did he not lose face, but he marked himself as a big man and both a great teacher and a true student. Socrates would have appreciated the exchange.

X

SETTLING IS FOR LAWYERS

Do not settle!

Some years ago Porsche produced a wonderful poster showing one of their cars and bearing the legend, "COMPROMISE IS FOR POLITICIANS". It is not surprising that many politicians are attorneys. Demand the best from yourself as well as from others. Do not live down to somebody else's expectations.

As long as you are going to make predictions, why not make them positive. When I first heard this simple statement some years ago, I was struck by the fact that I had lived so long without even considering this possibility.

It is far easier and much more destructive to make negative predictions about the future. It is one thing to assume that a final examination will be difficult and then to prepare well for it, and quite another to assume that you will do poorly on the test. In tests as in much of life there is a tendency toward self-fulfillment of prophecies.

Be true to yourself. Speak out! Listen! Read more! Do More! Learn more! Party more! Be more! Interesting, active and intelligent men and women are always in demand. So are good lookers, but outward appearances seem to count for less and less as people mature. Some people never mature.

Unlike stocks, bonds, and commodities, it is most difficult to profit from selling yourself short. I am talking about substance and not appearance. Some shrewd country lawyers have made their names and fortunes by beating their big city counterparts with good-old-boy appearances. Former Sen. Sam Ervin of North Carolina played this role like a master, but he was widely recognized as one of the nation's best constitutional lawyers.

Accepting less from yourself now means that you will be less later.

When non-lawyers talk about settling, what they usually mean is accepting less, being willing to take less or do poorer than they should. ("I'll bat out a paper tonight. It's no problem, because I'll do well on the final.") What we lawyers mean by settling is a different matter altogether. For a lawyer settling a case implies careful evaluation of the strengths and weaknesses of both sides of a dispute, the likely result of fully litigating the matter and the cost of litigating both in time and money in order to obtain the expected result. Lawyers also factor in the abilities of all counsel, the motivations of the parties, and the vagaries of judges and juries. All of this, attorneys call the "hazards of litigation". This is a lot different than merely accepting less.

Going out with someone other than Prince Charming is not settling, but staying in and moping while you wait for The Prince to come to your rescue may be. You may not recognize your prince when he finally comes unless you have learned along the way what qualities make your toad. Even so, today's toad may well be tomorrow's prince and today's prince almost certainly will be your toad sometimes. The babe in your life may just be a babe. You may very well prefer the scullery maid (who may or may not have a fairy godmother) to the princess.

You cannot fall in love. The Marriage Encounter movement teaches participants that, "Love is a decision." If you were able to fall in love, then just as easily you could fall out of love. Either way you would have no control over what happened to you. How do you feel about such lack of control? But, if instead, love is what you do (how you act), then you have the ability to decide to love or not to love. Either way you control what you do.

You would do well to delete the word "love" as a noun from your vocabulary and replace it with the verb "loving". (Use "I am loving you" instead of "I am in love with you".) My experience is that a person falls in love when he starts loving and that he falls out of love when he stops loving. Erich Fromm explains this much better than I do in his book, <u>To Have Or To Be</u>.

Make a list of all those books that you have read in the last three years without them having been assigned in school or used by you in research for school. If your list does not contain at least a dozen titles, you are not reading enough. If it contains only novels, only biographies or only books on one or two subjects, then you are not reading broadly enough. If you are not proud of your list, you are not reading enough of the right things for you.

You might also do well to make yourself a second working list of books you want to read for your own pleasure and enlightenment. You can add new titles at any time and remove titles as you read them or lose interest.

I was quite tempted to include my own lists at this point, but I could think of no good reason for doing so. Some of the books I have read recently already are mentioned in this book, but I did not write this book in order to get you to read all the books that I have read or that interest me. I am interested in getting you to read more of what will interest and stimulate you. On the other hand, I cannot help but believe that many of the books I mention will interest and stimulate you.

XI

LISTEN TO A DIFFERENT RADIO STATION

(With my apologies to Henry David Thoreau, who I have come to appreciate more and more as I mature.) For reasons that escape me Thoreau's <u>Walden</u> is usually assigned reading during the sophomore or junior years of high school, the very time when adolescents tend to place particular emphasis on peer group conformity. When I read <u>Walden</u> the first time for a high school English assignment, I did not appreciate it at all. If you have only read it once and did so in high school, be sure to read it again or at least add it to your list of books to read.

Conforming will turn you into one of the gang. Being yourself will enable you to be the unique individual you are. Be distinctive, but not weird. Write on the more obscure topic.

Any teacher will get tired and bored reading several papers on the same topic. Those at the end of the line might get short shrift. Those who write on distinctive and relevant topics are not required to stand in line.

Beth started to learn about writing on distinctive topics in high school, when she put off researching a history paper for so long that all of the materials on the "interesting" assigned optional topics had been checked out of both the school and local public libraries. (Believe it or not, some students fail to start projects promptly.) Grudgingly, thirty minutes before the library closed on the night before her paper was due, Beth telephoned me for help. I met her at the library and reviewed her list of topics. With ten minutes to go until closing, Beth resigned herself to writing her paper on the Renaissance Popes because I already had good source materials on this topic in my own library. After checking out a few additional volumes, Beth returned home and spent the entire night reading and writing. She was the only student in her class to write on this topic. Actually, in all the years that this course was offered she was the only student who ever wrote on this topic. She might have gotten her A anyway, but writing the only paper on a less sexy topic surely did not hurt.

Do the unexpected. Probe. Seek novel solutions by looking at problems in different ways. Today, many call this thinking outside the box. It seems to me that as soon as you say "the box" you have limited your options. Ask questions; specifically, ask new questions. Demonstrate an active interest in every class.
A woman named Beth McGreevy attending a Jewish event will stand out, even if she is Jewish. "Dumb jocks" who are smart stand out both in class and on the playing field. So do female engineering students, speech majors in economics classes, and white students in African history classes,

even if, as at some schools, they constitute a majority of the class. Except at a relatively small number of schools, native Americans always stand out. Sometimes standing out can backfire.

Most often I have found that being one of the crowd is a lot of fun socially but otherwise very confining. Take your pick.

Conformity in the classroom is another matter altogether. It may be that some of your elementary school or even high school teachers rewarded students who blended in. Some of mine did.

In eight years of undergraduate and graduate studies, though, I did not have even one professor who failed to look for and reward intellectual individuality. Conformity in the college classroom at best means mediocrity. For that matter conformity almost by definition means mediocrity. Average means so-so. Your point of reference is everything.

When I was in high school, I worked part-time in what we then called a record store, cassette tapes and CDs not yet having been invented. Part of my job was to keep track of record sales and report the top singles and LP's to <u>Billboard</u>, <u>Cashbox</u>, and one of the local radio stations. After a while I discovered that when it came to popular music, particularly rock and roll, the songs that made the charts were not necessarily the ones that people liked, but rather people tended to like the songs that were on the charts.

I remember one time when there was an unexpected delay in releasing a certain record into local stores for sale. Despite the fact that no store in our area had any copies available, it still made the local "Top 40" for reported sales.

XI

DO UNTO OTHERS

Being active almost always is better than being passive. <u>To Have Or To Be</u> by Erich Fromm ought to be required reading for every high school and college student. Being aware of the difference between knowing and having knowledge could make a profound difference in your academic life. Knowing the difference between loving and being in love will make a significant difference in your love life.

Write in the active mode. Observe carefully. Read everything you can. Exercise both your mind and your body. Initiate and do not just react. Attend all your classes.

I have noticed that those students who most seem to need to attend lectures often are the same ones who are most likely to skip them. Cause and effect may or may not be operational in this situation.

My brother, Kenneth Seeskin, who chairs the Department of Philosophy at Northwestern University, tells me that when he teaches Introduction To Philosophy, usually some student will approach him after one of his first lectures and ask if it is necessary to attend all his lectures. He says that he responds by asking the student about the university's current tuition rate. He then inquires about the proportion of that tuition that is applicable to his course.

He then tells the student that as he understands the situation, she or her parents have to pay the tuition whether or not she attends his lectures and that he will receive the same salary in either case. He then tells the student to do whatever she thinks is best.

Participate. Listen attentively. Be honest. I am not moralizing here. Those who are not honest with themselves and others are much more likely to enroll in courses they should not take, share rooms with incompatible roommates, plunge into bad relationships, and generally be more unhappy with their lives. Being truly honest may seem difficult, but see Chapter XXVII.

Think for yourself. Over the years I have read <u>The Art of Clear Thinking</u> by Rudolph Flesch half a dozen times. This marvelous book is out of print now, but if you can locate a copy and manage to get through the first several chapters, reading it will be well worth your while. Flesch's companion books, <u>The Art of Readable Writing</u> and <u>The Art of Plain Talk</u> are also worth reading.

Let your opinions be known. Challenge others. Accept other people as they are. If the difference between accepting people as they are and challenging their thinking is unclear to you, ask yourself if you always agree with the people you love.

Go. Do. Appreciate the eccentric both in yourself and in others.

Be a good roommate. This is true even if you are living alone. Actually, it is true particularly if you are living alone.

The trend in our modern society toward reading less and less has been well documented. Like most Americans, I probably watch far too much television. What I have noticed about myself, however, is that when I read more, read almost anything, I seem to feel better. What I read is essentially irrelevant in this regard, but the quality of what I read is important. It is most difficult to define "quality" but often I know it when I read it. See Robert Pirsig's Zen and the Art of Motorcycle Maintenance in which the protagonist struggles to discover the meaning of "quality".

If you believe that I am saying that reading causes me to feel better, you are wrong. I am not suggesting a cause and effect relationship. After all, I might read more because I feel better. If you do not understand what it means to say that for me reading more correlates with feeling better, you are missing a basic concept that you will need, no matter what you study and no matter what you do with your life.

In the past few years I have read several books by Arthur Train, including A Puritan's Progress and a book about Train's great literary hoax, titled Yankee Lawyer, Plato's The Republic, When Everything Changed by Gail Collins, a history of the Navajo Code Talkers of World War II, <u>Game Change</u>, Barbara Tuchman's <u>March of Folly</u>, (again) and a number of books on Judaism and the Jewish people.

When I first wrote the next paragraph in the draft that went to Beth, when she graduated from high school it read as follows:
> In the past few years I have read about half of the complete works of Earnest Hemingway, several good novels (including Nathaniel Hawthorne's <u>The Scarlet Letter</u>, which somehow I was never assigned to read in either high school or college courses in American literature!), <u>The Complete Sherlock Holmes</u>, a couple of plays, a history of the battle of Gettysburg, Barbara Tuchman's <u>March of Folly</u>, and a number of books on Judaism and the Jewish people.

If I had my way, every candidate for public office from Village Clerk to President would be required to certify as a precondition to entering the race that she has read <u>March of Folly</u>.

I have also read several critical evaluations of American schools and education (<u>Excellence</u> by John W. Gardner was written in 1961, but it is still so relevant that I recommended it to the president of our local school board), my brother's philosophical treatises on the Socratic Method and on Maimonides, some Confucius, a little poetry, some science fiction, a wide variety of articles on more subjects than I can begin to list here, a weekly news magazine, daily and weekly newspapers and two thoroughly trashy novels.

I also read <u>Swim with the Sharks Without Being Eaten Alive</u> by Harvey Mackay. If you have any interest concerning what it will take for you to succeed in your chosen field after graduation, get a copy of this book now. Mr. Mackay's company manufactures and sells envelopes, but his insights are hardly limited to that business. It is the first and only book of its kind that has provided me with both motivation and techniques for making some changes that I want for me in my life.

Beth gave Eileen and me a copy of Miss Manners' <u>Guide To Raising Perfect Children</u> as an anniversary present. After years of looking down on newspaper advice columnists, I began reading and appreciating Miss Manners' wit and wisdom; I loved every sentence. Give a copy of one of her books to your parents. They will thank you for your gift many times over and you can read it when you are at home.

Conversely, I have gone several years at a time without reading anything more than the minimum necessary at work and occasional glances at the newspaper. These periods were also the times when I was feeling the worst about myself and how well I was proceeding with making something of my life.

A few years ago I talked with the superintendent of our local public high school, by reputation one of the finest public schools in the country. He informed me that most of the college admissions officers that he talks to tell him that one of the most significant deficiencies that they see in recent applicants is their failure to do any significant amount of reading for pleasure.

QUESTION

The application for admission to college asks each applicant to identify an interesting book, not required in any class, he has read lately. You are the Director of Admissions at your college. Below are the answers of several applicants you will interview. Rank the applicants in the order of interest to you:
        A.   The latest Stephen King book;
        B.   Not sure;
        C.   <u>Moby Dick</u> by Herman Melville;
        D.   None;
        E.   <u>The Autobiography of Malcolm X</u>
Are you really interested in admitting anyone who answered B or D?

XIII

CALL OUT THE MARINES

When you need help, get it, as soon as you can, wherever you can, and however you can. Cheating is not getting help. Those who are unwilling to take responsibility for their own education are often unwilling to ask for help when they need it most.

I had the misfortune to whiz through high school on intellect alone. I started college with no real understanding of how to study and I paid dearly for my deficiency. After I managed to qualify for academic probation during my freshman year, my parents tried to help me by pointing out that I was smart enough. Either I was not studying enough, they said, or I was not studying correctly, or both. I assured them that I knew what I needed to do to get back on track even though I didn't have the foggiest notion of what I needed to do. Actually, at that time I had never been on track in the first place in college. Even worse, I knew that I didn't know what to do. Luckily for me, I found a right path in time, but others are not so fortunate.

Everybody gets stuck sometimes. More often than not, when you are stuck, any solution, any one at all, will be significantly better than the paralysis of not deciding on any solution.

You cannot delegate responsibility for you, but gutting it out alone is always the pits. There is no sick leave in college. Call or go home. Talk to your professors or teaching assistants. Ask classmates. See a counsellor. Inquire of anyone who might help. The school has an investment in your failure. If one person cannot or will not help you, ask another. The answer you seek is almost always in the library or more and more these days on the internet, and learning how to locate it is one of the most beneficial skills you can learn in college.

As a young child I quickly learned the importance of self-reliance. Unfortunately, I often carried this positive trait to such an extreme that I turned it into a defect. By not seeking assistance when I needed it and easily could have obtained it, I nearly flunked out of college during my freshman year, endangered my first marriage, spent many tortuous nights, and wasted a lot of time wallowing in self pity.

I suspect that my academic life would have been much different if I had admitted to my ninth grade Latin teacher that the way I was studying (or not studying) did not seem to be working for me and asked her for her help. In Miss Farrell's class **Veni, vidi, non vici.** I came, I saw, but I did not conquer.

Admitting to yourself and others that you need help in your educational, emotional, professional, or other development and knowing where and how to get the help you need is a sign of maturity and not weakness. The answer is not really always in the library or on the internet, particularly when it comes to developing your physical or artistic abilities, but they are great places for you to start looking.

You can **NEVER** underestimate the potential of a good used book store. If you delay starting your assignments long enough, like Beth and I used to do, you will probably find that by the time you get to the library, others have already checked out the key materials that you are seeking. Even if they have not, by checking out used book stores you may secure access to sources not considered by others.

In high school Jonathan's English teacher assigned Hemingway's <u>A Farewell To Arms</u>. I was not prepared to let him mark up my leather bound edition, so I took him to a used book store to purchase a cheap copy. Not only did we find several editions of the book, but also we discovered and purchased a book containing twenty critical essays on that masterpiece of American literature. We never checked, but I'm betting the school library doesn't have that volume.

XIV

A GOOD CIGAR IS A SMOKE

There will be plenty of geeks around you, but none of them will be stupid. When I was in college we called such people turkeys. Whatever the terminology it really says more about the attitudes of the speaker than the characteristics of the person described. Your classmates weren't admitted to college because they were cute. See Chapter I.

Every person has something unique to offer. Most men (women) are not for you, but some (not just one) are. If you look for the best in others, they will be more likely to discover the best in you. Keep your standards and be honest in all your relationships, but remember that a bad date is a bad date, but a good date is a good time. My friend, Vanda Jordan, once told my wife that when you want to say **"NO"**, you should say it and mean it, because when you do, your **"YES"** will mean so much more. Ray Robertson said the same thing. I don't know if Ray heard it from Vanda or the other way around.

If you are not yourself, who will she (he) like? If this sounds like pop psychology to you, read something by Father John Powell or Leo Buscaglia. If it does not, read some of their books anyway. Those of you searching for meaning in your studies will appreciate Buscaglia's story about driving through the Italian Alps. A young woman traveling in the opposite direction yelled at him "PIG!" in Italian as their cars passed. Buscaglia became angry at the woman. Within seconds he was steaming and almost hit the pig in the middle of the road as he rounded the next bend.

Every relationship will help you to define which qualities in another are truly important to you.

I attended the twenty-fifth reunion of my high school graduating class. I thoroughly enjoyed seeing old friends and learning about what they had done with their lives, how they had grown. Many of my classmates were now doing just about what I predicted. The editor of our school paper was publishing her own newspaper in Minneapolis. The president of our senior class was a judge (by our fortieth reunion he had become the mayor of a large city). One of the top two musicians taught music at Tulsa University and the other played in the Dallas Opera Symphony. Our math and science whiz was a big honcho for a computer firm in Denver.

There were a few surprises and what surprised me the most was how wrong I had been in making predictions about people I had viewed negatively in high school. They had gone on to be homemakers, police officers, small business owners, nurses, teachers, executives and professionals. They were raising families, educating their children, participating in a variety of activities in their communities and struggling with life's problems.

I suspect that my surprise was not caused so much by actual changes in my former classmates as it was by my earlier inability, or more likely my refusal, to see their many positive attributes. I am confident that I was no more blind than most of them.

[For any parents who might be reading this book, I am pleased to report that no one reacted negatively (only a little kidding) to my receding hairline and expanded waist. Learning that people I cared about and respected still cared about me as a person and not merely about my physical shape was most encouraging.]

The problem with not being yourself is that while others may be deceived by your acting, you will not be. Even worse, you will know that the person who the others like is someone else, not the real you. Of course, if others do not like the fake you, you can always seek comfort in believing that if only they knew the real you (which you will not permit), they would like you. Seeking acceptance necessarily includes the risk of being rejected.

XV

REMEMBER THE ALAMO!
OR IS IT THE MAINE?

Several years ago I read <u>Texas</u> by James Michener and I was reminded once again how much we are a product of the people and events that preceded us and how much better off we would be if we were more fully aware of that fact. That is a recurrent theme of Michener and appears in all of his multi-generation novels.

Remember everything you read and everything you hear because everything you learn is worth saving. If you cannot remember everything, learn to take good notes and keep good files. Keep in mind who you are, from where you came, and how you got to be the person you now are. The future never arrives. The past is alive. Savor the good times; be fully with the bad times. Learn from both your successes and your failures. What you know must be amended every so often.

Failures, bad times, hurt, and disappointments are all part of life. It is my experience that those people who tend to deny this are the ones most likely to seek escape in alcohol, illicit or prescribed drugs, work, etc.

Unfortunately, far too many parents seem to consider it one of their major parental duties to make sure that their children never learn to cope with such setbacks

If yours subscribe to this school of thought, I can offer you no help in changing them, but I urge you not to buy into their vision. On the other hand, you can be sure that problems will come your way without you looking for them. You do not have to be a masochist.

My parents used to tell me that suffering served the purpose of helping people to fully appreciate the good things in life. They were not advocating martyrdom, but only a recognition that despite what the old song says, life is not a bowl of cherries.

As a youth I quickly grew tired of hearing from my parents about the impact of the Great Depression on their lives. Still, I read The Day the Bubble Burst by Gordon Thomas and Max Morgan-Witts and heartily recommend it. Later I came to realize that the economic upheaval of the Thirties played no greater part in shaping their views of the world than did the political and social changes caused by the Civil Rights Movement and the war in Viet Nam for mine.

I have no idea which event will have such a great impact on your life that your children will grow tired of hearing you tell them about it. You can be sure, however, that such an event will occur, is now occurring, or already has occurred.

Some years ago, Eileen and I took Beth and Joel to see "Miss Saigon" when we were in London. Joel was spellbound. As we left the theater, he turned to us and asked "What was Viet Nam?" We were shocked, but quickly realized that what is still alive for products of the 60's is ancient history to their children. Wait until your children start asking you to tell them about how the presidential election of 2000 turned on about 500 disputed votes in Florida.

XVI

IT ALL DEPENDS ON HOW YOU LOOK AT IT

Keep everything in perspective. Context is always important. Set realistic goals for yourself and keep them in mind. If you want to take full advantage of goal setting, be sure to write yours down, keep your list and amend the list from time to time.

Evaluate honestly. There are at least three sides to almost every argument. If you are able to think of only two solutions to a problem, you are probably in deep trouble. Asking the proper question is the single most important step toward arriving at a correct answer. (Notice that I did not say "the correct answer".) Unless you are trying to decide whether to call heads or tails, a question in the form, "Should I ... or should I ...?" is likely to be a misleading question. Pigeon holes are for the birds.

Except in mathematics and multiple choice questions, there is probably more than one correct answer to every question. Even then sometimes there is more than one correct answer. There is always more than one way of determining the correct answer.

Do not be wishy-washy, but never make up your mind forever. An ostrich has trouble covering its ass.

"The word is not the thing; the map is not the territory." In college, while I was looking for an interesting filler course for what looked like a most difficult quarter, I blundered into an introductory course in general semantics, from which this concept has been lifted verbatim. Another important concept from general semantics is the notion that just because two things are called by the same name does not mean that those two things are the same.

I can think of no course I ever took in twenty-one years of formal schooling that I went into with less anticipation and came out of with more challenging new ideas and enthusiasm. If your college offers a course in general semantics, take it. If it doesn't, ask the Dean why it is not offered.

The concept of "The word is not the thing; the map is not the territory," seems simple enough, but it never ceases to surprise me how often even intelligent people confuse depiction of reality with reality.

On the first day in general semantics the professor placed a "lemon" on the podium. He then instructed each person to write down ten true statements about the item. He offered an A for the quarter to the first person who wrote down ten true statements. It turned out that the "lemon" was made of plastic, was hollow, and had a large cut-out facing away from the class. No one earned the A.

I remember reading a magazine article many

years ago about an experiment in which people were served perfectly good foods which had been dyed with tasteless coloring. (I understand that many food dyes are not good for you, but please bear with me.) Subjects were served green steak, blue potatoes, brown carrots, bright red lettuce, black milk, etc. I don't vouch for the actual colors, but you get the idea. The diners not only reacted negatively to the coloring, but invariably they also disliked the taste and aroma of the foods they were served. Control subjects were blindfolded, served the same foods and enjoyed their meals.

Most of us form initial opinions about people. Thereafter we see them in terms of those opinions and not as they really are. At some level this tendency is at the core of most racial and religious prejudice.

Even after going to my high school reunion, I still find it most difficult to picture my former classmates as I most recently saw them instead of how I remember them looking more than forty years ago.
Often we tend to react to mere labels without any attempt to find out if those labels are merited. When Joel started kindergarten in mid-year, a friend of his from day-care told him that Ms. O'Brien was a good teacher and that all the children in the class were nice, except for one boy. When Joel came home the first day, he promptly informed us that Ms. O'Brien was a good teacher and that

84

all the children in the class were nice, except for that one boy. Fortunately, within a few weeks Joel reconsidered and claimed that boy as a friend. Too often adults do more poorly at making up their own minds than do five year-old children.

Our reactions to people may be positive, negative, or neutral based only on their names (Eileen tells me that guys named Michael make good dates, but that a woman should look out for a David.), home towns (You know how New Yorkers are.), schools (You can always tell a Yale man.), clothes (which make the man), or body shapes (Fat people are jolly.). We often react to a person in a particular way simply because she reminds us of someone else. In so reacting we altogether miss the opportunity of knowing her as she really is.

We even tend to label ourselves and then to react to ourselves in terms of those labels. Having decided that we are preppies, we act like stereotypical preppies. Having labeled ourselves as punkers, we are sure to act like punks. Considering ourselves to be brains, we then carefully act as brains.

We have all heard about "dumb blondes" and "hot-tempered red heads", but I am aware of no evidence whatsoever which relates intelligence or temperament to hair color.

The so-called Socratic method of teaching by means of asking questions rather than lecturing is little used in undergraduate courses, not because of its failing but because it is much more difficult for a teacher to learn how to use it well. It is the method commonly used in law schools. It is not by coincidence that some have suggested that even if you do not want to be a lawyer, there is no way to obtain a better education in thinking on your feet.

In the hands of a master like Victor Rosenblum, professor of political science and law at Northwestern University, the Socratic method is a wonder to behold. As a sophomore I took a course called "Introduction To Law and Politics" which he taught. For an entire quarter all he did was ask questions and restate or summarize answers. Two years later, while doing an independent study with him, I decided that it would be helpful to me to sit in as an observer while he taught the class again. I found that by his asking questions (some the same and some different than he had asked two years previously), restating, and summarizing this class reached essentially the same conclusions as mine had. I no longer remember any of Professor Rosenblum's questions, but I do remember what I learned in his class.

Before Joel started kindergarten Eileen and I went to school to visit the class he would soon enter. Marge O'Brien was doing a much better job of teaching by questioning her five year-old students than almost all of the high school teachers and college professors with whom either Eileen or I had studied. Somewhere between kindergarten and law school the educational focus seemed to have shifted from the teacher asking questions and the student discovering his own answers to systematic inculcation.

This lack of clear thinking and all that goes with it has been described by Steve Allen, a recently deceased modern Renaissance man, as "dumbth". If you are starting college in the fall, if you already started college, if you have already graduated, or if you know someone who will go, is going, or has gone to college, then read his exciting book, <u>Dumbth and 81 Ways To Make Americans Smarter</u>. (If you are not sure just what it means to be a "Renaissance man," then it is even more important that you read Allen's book.

XVII

TIME FLIES WHEN YOU ARE HAVING FUN

The amount of time you will require to complete your homework will vary from school to school and from course to course, but the principles stated below remain the same. Learning to pace yourself will make academic life easier for you and enable you to learn more.

Every hour that you spend in class will probably require that you spend an average of about three hours doing homework outside of the classroom. A week before I first wrote this Joel, Eileen, and I returned from a "Preview" session at Illinois State University where Joel was about to enroll. In one of the sessions, an academic advisor told us that students should plan on 2 1/2 to 3 hours of homework per class hour. Whether it's 2 1/2 hours or 3 hours or some other number of hours, you have to study as long as necessary. What takes your classmate 2 hours may take you 4. Focus on the concept rather than the numbers.

"Average" means "more" about half the time. If you choose to, you can substitute "median", but I suspect that the average (mean) and the median are about the same.
In Jonathan's freshman seminar he was required to read several original source books on slavery and freedom in America. The first week's text was only about 100 pages long. The second week he read a 300 page book, and the third week he read 650 pages. On average he read 350 pages a week, but that would not have been helpful in planning his studies for the first or third weeks.

Thinking of averages, I am reminded of a story about two duck hunters spending their pre-dawn hours in a rough blind. When the first ducks appear the more experienced shooter waits for the right time. The novice, however, gets off four quick shots. The first is in front of a duck and the second behind it. The third goes over the duck. The last shot is under the duck, but as the bullet goes by, the duck falls dead. The first hunter expresses total disbelief. The other replies, "I just shoot as best I can. The law of averages takes care of the duck."

Spending fifteen hours in class each week means that you will have an average sixty hour education week (fifteen hours in class and forty-five hours of homework). Spreading forty-five hours of homework evenly over a full week requires only 6.4 hours of study a day. Goofing off for one day and doing the work over the remaining six makes it 7.5 hours of study per day, which is still less than a typical work day.
Taking off the full weekend for fun means that to complete your week's work will require a full nine hours of study per weekday. Doing all the necessary work in only four days will require an effort of 11.25 hours per day in addition to attending classes, eating meals, dressing, brushing your teeth, etc. Cramming your studying into three days will take fifteen hours per day. Trying to do it in two days requires that you go "Back To The Future".

If your education requires only two hours of outside work for each hour in class, the above numbers will change, but the principle will remain exactly the same. See Chapters IV and V.

My experience is that in actual practice these figures often are meaningless. Those college students who spend their entire weekends engaged in non-academic pursuits actually are more likely to spend less time studying during the week than those who hit the books on Saturday and Sunday. It seems to me that only those students who manage their time well actually devote enough time to their studies. Effective time management is even more important for those students involved in non-academic activities requiring significant blocks of time. The numbers may change but the principles are the same for athletes, debaters, band members, newspaper reporters, and student politicians, to say nothing of the many students who also work at part-time jobs.

During my undergraduate years I sold football programs, bussed tables, taught swimming, and supervised a variety of park district events. Beth rebound books, provided security in a campus art gallery, and served pizzas. Aaron taught Sunday school, provided security in a residence hall, and proctored a computer laboratory from midnight to 8:00 a.m. on Tuesday mornings. Jonathan started doing office work at the Traffic Institute and later worked in a campus coffee house. Going off to college Joel hoped to land a job at the campus bowling and billiard center. He didn't get the job and hasn't worked while in school, but when home he has worked for the local park district, made popcorn, delivered pizza, supervised sports activities at a day camp, and umpired youth baseball games. With the changing time commitments of these jobs each of us had to adjust our respective schedules.

An hour spent studying counts for a full hour only if the entire hour is utilized completely. You cannot include late starts or early finishes; 7:05 to 7:55 amounts to only fifty minutes, not an hour. Time used talking on the telephone is not being used to study. Bathroom trips, snack breaks, and time spent staring at a paragraph or a photograph do not count. Neither does time spent sharpening pencils, daydreaming, socializing, kibitzing, reading other materials, writing letters, watching television, listening to the radio, or changing CDs.

After putting myself into a severe academic hole in college, I decided to keep a diary of all of my activities for an entire week in order to learn how I was really utilizing my time. I was quite surprised to discover that my actual studying time amounted to only about half of the time that I previously had attributed to studying. I also learned that I had grossly underestimated the amount of time that I considered wasted. Armed with this information, improving my study habits primarily amounted to reducing the amount of time that I myself considered wasted.

My brother Ken used to say that he hated to work and that was the reason he had become a professor. Claiming that he only taught a few hours a week, he steadfastly refused to count the many hours he spent reading, doing research, writing articles, and preparing his lectures. Professors have a lot more homework to do than any of their students.

If you become sufficiently interested in your studies, the time that you spend studying will seem less like work and much more like pleasure. In an introductory Russian literature course I was assigned to read during one week Dostoevski's masterpiece, <u>Crime and Punishment</u>. I read it in one sitting. No one could ever convince me that I spent the time doing homework. That classic book may not be as enjoyable to you, but there are many courses and many books at which I had to work hard that you may simply enjoy.

XVIII

NO TRIAL IS AN ERROR

A person at rest tends to remain at rest (depression); A person in motion tends to remain in motion (growth). Stop and go people (bipolar) waste energy. The laws of physics apply to people also.

If you do not make an effort, you cannot succeed at anything. But saying that you are trying to do something usually is nothing more than an excuse for not doing it. Think about the real difference between "I am studying" and "I am trying to study." The distinction is clear. The difference between "I am doing my best" and "I am trying to do my best" is no less clear. Stop saying that you are trying to do something and you will likely start to accomplish more while making fewer excuses.

When one of his patients would tell Ray Robertson that she was trying to do something, Ray usually replied that he would try to be a good therapist for her. Needless to say, none of Ray's patients was willing to settle merely for his attempts.

The greater the risk involved, the greater is your potential reward. There is no success in a sure thing.

As a lawyer I have learned that I get the most satisfaction from doing work that someone else probably would not have done as well and from obtaining results that might easily have been missed but for my efforts. Filling out pre-printed forms, obtaining default judgments and other "sure (legal) things" are necessary parts of my job, but they hardly help me to feel good about being an attorney.

Years ago I went to the cinema to see "The Breakfast Club", a movie greatly loved by adolescents and pre-adolescents about misunderstood and mistreated teenagers unwilling to take responsibility for themselves. Fortunately, I chose to attend a theater showing a sneak preview as a double feature. (!)

The second movie was called "the Sure Thing", a surprisingly good but commercially less successful film about an east coast college man who travels completely across country during a school break for a date with a woman, who a friend has guaranteed to be a "sure (sexual) thing". Not surprisingly, he finds that when he meets the young lady, she truly is a "sure thing" but that despite that, or more likely because of that, he really does not want to be with her. The woman he really wants to be with is the one he has traveled and battled with on the drive west.

As I was writing this chapter I began to think how much more interesting the story would have been from the viewpoint of the young lady, but with a twist. For most of the movie she does her best to avoid the not-so-cool guy in her literature class while waiting for the "sure thing" to arrive. When he does arrive, he is the ultimate hunk and he reeks of Valentino, about to sweep her off her feet and ride off with her into the sunset. At the last second she turns him down and goes off with the guy next door.

Anyway, all this tends to confirm that in making movies for profit, one of the sure things is to make a film about misunderstood teenagers. Films about misunderstanding teenagers do not sell as well.

XIX

YOU'RE IN THE ARMY NOW

Nobody promised you that college would be all fun and games. In fact, you were told in the clearest terms that it would not be. Doing well in college takes more than study. It will require that you take courses you would prefer to work your way around, listen to professors you would happily dismiss, read books you would rather miss, and write papers you would rather avoid.

Of course, when you are all through (whenever that may be), you may be glad that you took that course, paid heed to that professor, read that book, and wrote that paper. The computer rule of GIGO (Garbage In, Garbage Out) probably applies here, but there is a lot less GI in college than most students believe. To make matters worse, it is most difficult to determine from the perspective of the student what really is GI. Your reluctance or even resistance, going in may rapidly convert to acceptance, if not outright enthusiasm, coming out.

Doing well in college also means skipping parties that you planned to attend, missing sporting and cultural events that you looked forward to, and not spending as much time as you want to with people you like. When necessary, soldier and do what you have to do, whether or not you like it and whether or not you see the benefit.

You will never get everything you want, but you are entitled to want nevertheless.

Some of this may sound extremely unattractive to you, but your years in college will probably provide some of the best times of your life. Actually, years from now when you look back on the hard times or even the bad times, you will probably miss those times. Sadly, too many students stress all those good times, forget the real reasons they are in college, drop out of school, and paradoxically miss most of the best times.

Soldiering means doing what you must do, whether or not you want to do it. Everybody has to soldier some of the time. Nobody gets her way all of the time. Soldiering involves more, however. It also requires that you do what you must do without griping and bitterness. A crisp "Yes, sir" or "No, Ma'am" probably will suffice.

Children sometimes have to soldier and so do their parents. Employees sometimes have to soldier and so do their bosses. Students sometimes have to soldier and so do their teachers. Learning how to soldier with style will go a long way toward helping you reach your goal.

XX

LET THE GOOD TIMES ROLL!

Bookworms eat paper. Wallflowers only

hang around. Participation is its own reward. Party until you feel good. Let others know the silly you. For that matter, be sure that you know the silly you. Dance the night away. Make mistakes.

While I was on vacation a few years ago, I discovered, purchased, and gave to Aaron a delightful poster that listed "Murphy's Computer Laws" that included one that read something like, "Judgment comes from experience; experience comes from faulty judgment." Even Murphy understands that we can and must learn from our mistakes.

In his acceptance speech at the 1992 Republican National Convention, President George Bush (the father) cited Murphy in support of his position that he had made a mistake in reneging on his "Read my lips, no new taxes" pledge. I thought that this explanation was the best part of his speech.

Loll on the beach. Play in the snow. Listen to the music. Eat well. Sleep late. Hit the slopes. Laugh until your sides hurt good. Let yourself go. Watch the sunrise. Make your own list.

Your primary reason for going to college must always be to obtain a formal education, but if that is your only reason, then your college experience will come up short. You can learn in the library, but you will need much broader vistas to discover who you really are and where you are going. Learning about yourself can be done only in part through academic study; the balance must come from experience.

When I went to Northwestern, men lived on north campus and women lived on south campus. By the time Beth arrived at the same school twenty-six years later, she had to go through a men's suite in her dorm in order to get to her room.

I do not believe that sexual activity and success in college correlate one way or the other. I do believe, however, that young people who make decisions concerning their sexual activities or lack of activity for the wrong reasons (i.e. fear, rebellion, conformity, etc.) are much more likely to be making other decisions for the wrong reasons and less likely to be doing as well as they might in college.

The decision to become sexually active is a very personal one. It is not my intent to tell you what you should or should not do in this regard. There will be plenty of other people ready and willing (able or not) to tell you what you should do about sexual activity.

Nevertheless, I firmly believe that any college student who engages in unsafe sex should be expelled from school for having demonstrated such poor thought processes as to prove that he or she doesn't belong in college.

Unlike Professor Harold Hill, "The Music Man", I do not consider that the (very few) hours I have spent with a pool cue in my hand have been golden. However, I have discovered a lot about myself at the bridge table, on intramural football fields, at the theatre, in late night/early morning dorm discussions, at fraternity parties, in various automobiles, in the bleachers at sporting events, and in the pages of untold numbers of books. I would not trade those experiences for anything.

XXI

WHAT YOU GET IS WHAT YOU SEE

When you are doing research, remember that primary sources are always better than secondary sources. Secondary sources in turn are always better than tertiary sources. Tertiary sources are acceptable, but the least preferred.

Encyclopedia and canned course and book outlines are not sources at all, but that does not mean that they will be totally useless to you. My experience is that most students who use "Cliff Notes" and the like tend to rely on them too heavily. Even for history and journalism majors, college is more about thinking than reporting.

What I have said about encyclopedia and canned outlines is not true, of course (they are secondary or tertiary sources), but you should assume that your professors mistakenly believe that it is true. If you get the chance, read "Hymn To The Truth", (<u>Prejudices: Sixth Series</u>), H. L. Mencken's serious account of how his completely fictitious humorous essay on the history of the bathtub came to be accepted as fact and ultimately was reported in learned journals and standard reference works, including <u>Encyclopedia Britannica</u>. As strange as that was, the difficulties that Mencken later encountered in convincing the so-called authorities that his original essay had been satirical and not the "truth" was even more amazing.

Mencken's experience was not unique. For years Arthur Train wrote short stories about the lovable fictional attorney, Ephraim Tutt. Eventually he wrote "Yankee Lawyer, The Autobiography of Ephraim Tutt". So many people wrote to Tutt seeking legal advice, that Train felt compelled to write a piece setting the record straight. It was no help. To this day the "Autobiography" is generally sold as non-fiction, often as the story of the "real" Ephraim Tutt, upon whom Arthur Train "based his fictional character."

No source will ever replace clear independent thinking. Totally independent clear thinking not based on sources of some kind is virtually impossible.

Primary sources are original documents, including for most undergraduate purposes copies and verbatim recordings of documents.

If your research topic had to do with the text of President Lincoln's Gettysburg address, then any verbatim text of his speech would be an original source document. If, instead, your research had to do with Nineteenth Century handwriting styles, then a mere verbatim text would be useless, but a photocopy of Lincoln's original hand-written manuscript would be an original source document. But if your research concerned a comparison of changing characteristics of parchments and papers, then only the original manuscript itself or a copy produced at about the same time would be an original.

Secondary sources restate, examine, explain, evaluate, compare, contrast, translate or criticize primary sources. Tertiary sources in turn restate, examine, explain, evaluate, compare, contrast, translate or criticize secondary sources. Sources that restate, examine, explain, evaluate, compare, contrast, translate or criticize tertiary sources generally are still called tertiary sources.

For example, in researching acceptable limitations on Speech protected under the First Amendment to the United States Constitution, the Constitution and its amendments or verbatim copies would be primary sources, an original commentary, such as The Federalist, would be a secondary source, and an article based on The Federalist would be a tertiary source.

For research concerning reactions to the proposed First Amendment at the time it was drafted, however, The Federalist, would be a primary source and an article based on it would be a secondary source. Finally, if the topic under consideration was how scholarly interpretations of the significance of The Federalist have changed over the years, the article in turn would be a primary source.

These important distinctions are not always so obvious. A student in a comparative religion class writing on the meaning of a particular Old Testament passage might turn to her family Bible, thinking that she was using a primary source. She would be in error because her English Bible would be either a secondary source (a translation directly from the original Hebrew) or a tertiary source (a translation from a language such as Latin or ancient Greek, which in turn was a translation from the original Hebrew. Of course, if she didn't know Latin, ancient Greek or Hebrew, this tertiary source might be the best source available to her.

The problem is illustrated by the thirty-first chapter of the book of Proverbs, which in Hebrew begins with the words "Eshet Chayil". (pronounced "chaiyil") Christians often translate these words as "A woman of virtue" (moral excellence, goodness, righteousness), although I have also seen Christian translations of "A good woman", "A woman of good character", and "A woman of noble character". Jews tend to translate the same Hebrew as "A woman of valor" (boldness or determination in facing great danger, especially in battle; heroic courage), a very different concept.

Not surprisingly the usual Jewish translation (secondary) comes closer in meaning than the usual Christian translation (tertiary), although when one looks at the original (primary) neither translation completely fits the meaning. Rabbi W. Gunther Plaut has come closer to the meaning of the Hebrew. He says that the woman described is "practical" with

104

"her feet planted firmly on the ground". "(S)he works hard for (her) husband and household, she is provident and thrifty." She has an "inner strength which permeates her labors and her home." [2]

An even better idea of the real meaning can be obtained by looking at several Hebrew idioms that include the word "chail"). Their translations (?) include "to muster strength", "warrior" or "fighter", "from strength to strength", "infantry", "navy", "armored corps", and "air force", "garrison", "to do well" or "prosper", "labor pains", and "fear and trembling". Finally, the word "chail" is itself an extension of the root word "chai", which means "living", "alive" or "lively".

Christian Biblical scholars are aware of this problem in translation and often learn Hebrew in order to base their research on original source material.

Keeping these distinctions in mind will help you when you are developing your own research topics and writing papers based on that research. My experience is that professors generally place the highest value on original work (i.e. new research, independent thinking, creative writing, artistic expression, etc.). Secondary work (i.e. examination, translation, explanation, evaluation, comparison,

---

[2]Plaut, W. Gunther, "The Book of Proverbs, A Commentary", UAHC, New York, 1961.

interpretation, contrast or criticism of another's original [primary] work) is valued next highest. Tertiary work is the least appreciated, but by far it is the most common.

Strangely, a good number, if not most, of the text books that you will use in college will be tertiary documents.

XXII

REACH FOR THE BRASS RING
(GO FOR THE GUSTO)

Listen carefully to what teachers and other students have to say about courses, schedules, professors, etc., but do not accept anybody's word, including mine, as being completely accurate. Remember that I went to college years ago and unless you happen to be attending Northwestern or George Washington, it was not your school. Your teachers and classmates have interests, abilities and viewpoints which likely differ from yours.

Easy (when I went to college we tended to call them "Mickey Mouse") classes generally should be avoided, because you will not have as much to learn. More difficult courses will be challenging and you will have the opportunity to learn more.

I understand that you have to be realistic. Taking two excellent literature courses at the same time may involve too much reading for you. Likewise, there may be an absolute limit on the number of laboratory experiments that you can conduct and write up during the same term.

My understanding is pretty much academic, however. My experience is that for most undergraduate students the tendency to do as little as possible for as long as possible. Very few students really bite off more than they can chew.

Taking a risk can be dangerous, but refusing to take any risks at all surely will be even more dangerous.

Good art is a thing to behold. Good literature is universal. Good music plays forever. Great professors are a joy. Sleep is necessary, even for modern Edisons. Hard work is invigorating. Wild parties are a must. Relaxation is essential. Sharing life with good friends will improve everything. Solitude clarifies. Sometimes you miss. See Chapter II.

Courses taken by large numbers of non-majors as electives tend to be worth your effort. When a course is taught by different professors at different times or during different terms and one professor regularly has more students enrolled, it is probably because she is a better teacher.

If a non-required course that sounds uninteresting or odd is offered in a large lecture hall, do not miss it. My university offered a course called Introduction To History of the American West, lovingly referred to by students as "Cowboys and Indians". It was regularly offered in the largest lecture hall on campus and enrollment was always limited by the number of available seats. When the professor, moved on to become a fellow at a noted private research library, the school continued to offer the course, but with a different professor. He drew substantially fewer students. I heard that the replacement professor teaching the course was good, but ....

Better courses taught by better professors will probably mean more work for you, but the rewards almost always will be worth your added effort. You will have no more important research to do in college than to obtain the information you need to select the best courses and professors for you.

Watch for late changes to the list of available courses. Jonathan was in one of the last groups to enroll for classes during his first quarter. He was worried about getting into one of the freshman seminars that he preferred. Despite the fact that he was one of the last to register, he wound up getting his first choice, a seminar that was added after the list of courses offered was distributed. On the other hand, he made a great effort to get into a particular calculus class because of its time and location. Unfortunately for him, he missed the fact that the class had been moved from one end of campus to the other.

Good books tend to drive out bad. This works in a manner opposite to Gresham's law, that "Bad money drives out good." If you do not understand what Gresham meant, start looking through your change and see how many silver quarters as opposed to aluminum clad copper coins you find.

Given the vast number of truly bad novels

and "kiss and tell" biographies that crowd book store shelves, you may be tempted to doubt what I say, but note how quickly most of them disappear, while really good books are always available. I think that all those bad books are testimony to the large portion of the population who have never read a good book.

Good literature is addictive in that every time you read something good you enhance your appetite for reading more good literature. The academic world is currently in the midst of a debate between those who believe that students should read great literature as our society knows and has known it and those who believe that what we have defined as "great literature" all too often has been "white, male, Western literature". As a college student I would have been squarely with the traditionalists, but I am moving to the other side now. In any case, for me the answer is not to read something different, but to read more and read more broadly.

To this day I find it shocking that although I came of age along with the Civil Rights Movement in the 60's, it wasn't until I was twenty-six years old and enrolled in a post-graduate legal program that I read anything by Frederick Douglass, Marcus Garvey or W. E. B. DuBois. Just as frightening for me was that I was almost fifty years old before I even heard of "A Vindication of the Rights of Woman" by Mary Wollstonecraft.

110

A book is good if some part of you wants to read it again. A book is good if you want to talk about it with someone else who has read it. A book is good if you recommend it to someone else who has not read it, hoping that you can discuss it with that person later. A book is good if it leaves you with questions that you want answered. For me a book is good if I want a leather-bound copy to add to my library.

Similarly, a professor is good if some part of you wants to hear her lectures again. A professor is good if you want to talk about his lectures with someone else in the class. A professor is good if you are willing to recommend her class to someone else who has not yet taken it, hoping that you can discuss her lectures with that person later. A professor is good if he leaves you with questions that you want answered.

A book probably is not good if you cannot remember its title or author. A book is not good if it fails to give you some new insights. A book is not good if it fails to leave you with questions that you want answered.

Whether or not a book is good does not depend on the extent to which you agree with the author. In fact, a good argument can be made that truly good books always break new ground.
Of course, that does not mean that books that break new ground are necessarily readable.

A while ago a friend and her three-year old visited us. The child grew restless while her mother talked with my wife. I placed the young girl on my lap, grabbed a book from the adjacent shelf, opened it to the first page and started to read. The book I grabbed was Albert Einstein's "The Meaning of Relativity". Before I had finished two sentences, the girl was snoozing. Try as I might, I couldn't finish the first paragraph.

XXIII

THE WHOLE IS GREATER THAN THE SUM OF ITS PARTS

The various courses that you will take in college will cover individual subjects, but with only a few exceptions the most important things for you to learn in college will not be dealt with directly in any single course or even in a series of courses. Some of the most important things that you will need to learn in college, in the order that I thought of them, are:

To be aware;

To appreciate and understand the world around you;

To be creative;

To think clearly and on your feet;

To communicate clearly and accurately;

To know and appreciate yourself;

To be inquisitive;

To learn how to learn;

To learn how to find what you need to know or want to know;

To appreciate the value of ideas and beliefs you do not share;

To rid yourself of bias and intolerance;

To expand your knowledge and awareness;

To make decisions;

To understand who you are;

To know what is worth remembering and to remember it;

To make reasonable predictions based

on too little information;

To see the world through someone else's eyes; and

To acquire and develop the skills you will need.

Be skeptical of claims that a list is in "no particular order." Obtaining true randomness is most difficult. I am sure that there is some definite order to my list, but I don't know what it is.

Keep in mind that the task of learning these things or for that matter, learning anything else never will be truly completed, either while you are in college or after you graduate. Like life, learning is a journey; it is not a destination.

I never got an "A" from Paul Schilpp. I wrote to him on the occasion of his ninetieth birthday. When I received his kind reply, I felt as if I had received an A from him on a midterm exam. It was then that I realized most clearly that almost thirty years previously, while I had been studying what the great philosophers of the past had written about ethics, he was more concerned with what I was doing about developing my own ethical concepts.

The great thinkers of the past were there only to serve as guides for me, but I did not fully appreciate that as a student. The truth of the matter is that I never deserved an "A" in class from Paul Schilpp, but I would like to think that I am earning my true grade now.

XXIV

GET THE SMALL PICTURE
DON'T MISS THE TREES FOR THE FOREST

All of the little things will add up. Having a good overview is always important, but often the details will make the difference between doing well and merely getting by. Being cutesy is never impressive in an academic setting. Do not bother wondering how I define "cutesy". You know it when you do it.

There is no such thing as a good paper with misspelled words, bad grammar, non-parallel constructions, improper syntax, or incorrect verb tenses.

If you do not believe this, you need a teacher such as Arthur Levin, who taught me journalism in high school, and recently retired as a professor at Butler University. He taught his students so well that seven different times the "Proviso West Profile", the school newspaper that he served as adviser, was selected by professional journalists as one of the five best high school newspapers in the country.

Names, dates, places, titles, figures, etc., are always important. If you do not have perfect recall, you will just have to work harder at memorizing all of those things that you need to remember in order to do well. Better yet, you can learn how to access what you need.

I have known a couple of people with so-called photographic memories. Their perfect recall did not always enhance their creative and thought processes. In fact, I suspect that sometimes it interfered.

Memory is a selective thing. Almost forty years ago I took an introductory course in physical geography, which required that I memorize several hundred of the world's geographic features by name, location and significance. As final exam week approached and my classmates were spending long hours memorizing lengthy and complicated lists of mountain ranges, lakes, rivers and the like, I discovered that with the exception of only about ten features I had retained all of the material from my reviews as the course proceeded. As good as my memory was for physical geography, it was that bad in Spanish.

Now, many years later I still remember that one of the country's most important copper mining areas is near Bisbee, Arizona and that a kame is a circular glacio-fluvial mound, both irrelevant facts for me.

On the other hand, I have long since forgotten almost all of the Spanish I learned in college. I could have used fluency in Spanish to my personal and business advantage many times since my graduation from college. Clearly, had I been able to predict the future more accurately, I would have learned Spanish a lot better. Sometimes it is hard to tell what will be relevant.

Knowing the reasons for your selective memory will not be as important to you as just being aware that it exists. Some materials will be more difficult for you to learn, and other materials will be much easier. It will take more time and harder work to master the materials in one course and less time and easier work in another. Do not waste your time attempting to figure out why.

XXV

LET THEM EAT CAKE

Determining what each of your professors expects from you is an integral part of your college education. If he wants original thinking, be creative. If she wants you to learn details, memorize everything. If he wants an overview, soar. If she wants class participation, speak out. If he wants bullshit, shovel it with a smile. Even when the professor is wrong, she is right, ... unless she changes her mind.

I first learned that teachers are always right from my mother as applied to elementary school teachers. My mother was wrong, but with only a few exceptions, you will be much better off if you act as if she was correct. If your actions will be inconsistent with your thoughts, go with the former, but if it is a matter of principle for you and you are willing to risk the consequences, then do what you think is right. Being true to your ethical belief is always important, but not every choice that you must make involves an ethical decision. When your professor "suggests" that you rewrite a piece, don't try to confuse improving your writing skills with violating creative license. The poet E. E. Cummings wrote much of his work without capital letters or punctuation, but you can be sure that early on he learned all the applicable rules that he later chose to ignore.

In my first draft of this book I wrote that I suspected that the odds of winning the state lottery were generous when compared to the chances of convincing a professor that his expectations of his students were in error. Upon giving thought to the matter I later decided that I had overstated the case.

The first mid-term examination I faced in college was in Introduction to American Government and Politics, the initial course for my planned political science major. I was devastated when I received a D.

In retrospect I know that I had not studied correctly or long enough for that exam. I also wasted time while taking the test trying to figure out the professor's little joke in asking for a short paragraph identifying "Learned Foote". The only person I had ever heard of with the first name of Learned was Learned Hand, probably the most outstanding jurist this country has ever produced, who never served on the Supreme Court. I couldn't imagine that the professor's humor would be so evident and wasted precious time trying to decide what to do.

At the next lecture the professor, Victor Rosenblum, announced that a particularly large number of students had done poorly on the mid-term. He said that he could think of only three possible explanations: the admissions office had lowered its standards without letting the faculty know it was doing so, he wasn't as good a teacher as he liked to believe, or he had written a poor set of examination questions.

Stating that he had no evidence whatsoever to support the first possibility and that he was loath to even consider the second, he tentatively placed the blame on the examination. All those students who received a D or an F on the first mid-term were given the opportunity to repeat the exam with new questions. Given a rare second chance, I got a B+ the next time around.

Come to think of it, maybe my first estimate of the odds was the correct one.

XXVI

JUMPING THE GUN IS NOT A FALSE START

Getting a college education may take you four years or longer, but it is more like running a series of dashes (sort of like intellectual interval training) than a marathon. With only a very few exceptions, within the first few days after the start of your freshman year, those students who will do well in college will already have gotten a fast start and distanced themselves from the majority of their classmates, who will merely get by. Even if you don't believe me, you will be much better off if you pretend as if you do.

About two months before he left for Illinois State University, Joel received a letter from the directors of a course titled "Foundations of Inquiry" that was required of all Freshmen. The class, intended to help in the transition from high school to college, was taught in small sections by about a hundred faculty members. Each section involved a different subject area, but the universals being taught had to do with critical reading, appropriate reasoning, and cogent argumentation.

The letter contained a list of five books for "suggested" reading during the summer. At first, Joel's response was that the reading was "only suggested". After rethinking the matter, he decided that he ought to heed the suggestion. By the time classes started those students who took the "suggestion" and read the books had already gotten a fast start and distanced themselves from their classmates who didn't read the "suggested" books.

The most recent information that I have seen indicates that almost 90% of all college students earn lower grades than they did in high school. Doing things the way you did them in high school will keep you in the majority. Doing as well or better than you did in high school requires that you make an active decision to succeed and that you make a daily reaffirmation of that decision.

In those same first few days of the first term those students who will merely fill out the class or ultimately drop out of school altogether will already have fallen behind. The belief that you can come on strong to win in the home stretch is an illusion.

There will never be enough time to prepare for exams for which you **must** study; there always will be enough time to study for exams for which you have been preparing all term. See Chapters V, VI and XVII.

Check for your assignments prior to the first class meeting. New Student Week can be a valuable experience, but you will do well to end yours a day early and devote yourself to preparing for the classes to come. You will probably miss a party, but that will be a small price to pay for the advantage you will gain. Too many students are unable to differentiate between the end of New Student Week and the beginning of the term. See Chapter XVII.

Obtain an assignment book or Palm Pilot for keeping track of your academic calendar and assignments. Familiarize yourself with your assigned texts. Begin your reading. Plan ahead. Start on longer term projects at once, if only to begin thinking about them. Establish your class and study schedules and allow yourself absolutely no variations at the start of your college career.

Study dates during your first few weeks of classes should be avoided. Once your good study patterns are well developed, however, I heartily recommend them.

Most students first entering college will passively decide to ease into their studies. By the time they fully acclimate themselves to their new educational environment they will be behind forever. Those students who actively decide to hit the ground running will quickly gain a head start that they seldom will lose. There are many fewer exceptions to this rule than you would like to believe.

Obtaining all of your textbooks and supplies before your classes start is essential. You may be surprised to learn that book stores at just about every college in the country fail to order and obtain sufficient books for all students in every course. I have absolutely no factual basis whatsoever for making this statement. On the other hand, I have yet to meet a college student, past or present, who never had a problem obtaining all his assigned texts.

The later you first attempt to buy your textbooks, the more likely it will be that your particular courses will be the ones with back orders or shortfalls (another of Murphy's Laws). Used books are cheaper, but make sure that you obtain the correct editions. Even if you cannot purchase your own texts, remember that copies of most assigned books will be on reserve in the library, but other students will be looking there too.

XXVII

"JEOPARDESE" IS SPOKEN HERE

When you sit down to take any examination, you should already know which questions will be on the test. If you do not, then you have not properly prepared yourself. Please note that I am not saying that you will know the answers (which you should), but that you should know the **questions**. In math and science courses you may not know the specific numbers, but the types of problems that will be on the exam should be obvious.

For those students who listen and study properly there are never surprise questions on exams. Professors are predictable. Now and then a professor with a sense of humor will include a truly surprise question on a test, but hardly anybody will know the answer.

In a class in Comparative Political Systems, my professor, R. Barry Farrell, asked for a short paragraph identifying Karl Friederich Goerdler, who had never been mentioned in lectures and referred to only in passing in one of the nine or ten assigned texts as being one of the people who "also" attended a certain meeting in Nazi Germany. No one knew the answer, so nobody suffered. For some reason I still remember Mr. Goerdler's name, if not which meeting he attended.

Professors only assign good books because

they only assign books that they think are worth reading. If you disagree, keep your opinions to yourself. It is one thing to tell your American Literature professor that the author he considers the most important of the century ranks only second on your list. It is quite another to tell her that the author she values is the most overrated writer of all times. You may be correct, but do yourself a favor and wait until you no longer need anything (grade, recommendation, approval, consent, etc.) from her.

I write from experience. In freshman English I didn't appreciate Henry James' <u>Portrait of a Lady</u> and told the professor why in a no-holds-barred paper. By his grading and comments he let me know why he appreciated the book as "one of the greatest masterpieces of American literature."

A good night's sleep leads to better examination answers.

The professor's question is only a jumping off point for your answer. There is no correct answer to any essay question. There are, however, many ways to properly write an answer.

There are an infinite number of wrong answers for every exam question. Supporting your position counts more than the position being supported. Take home examinations always require much more planning and thought. An open book exam is a trap designed to lull you into unwarranted confidence. If you have prepared yourself well, there is no such thing as a difficult exam, but there are easy exams.

Every professor from whom I ever took a course gave me plenty of advance notice of all of the examination questions. Unfortunately, like most of my fellow students, I was not always alert enough to recognize those notices for what they were.

Statements in lectures that someone or something is the best, the most important, the most misunderstood, the least appreciated, the most overrated, etc. are clear signals for future exam questions. Treat all superlatives from the professor as if they were in all capital letters, boldfaced and underlined. Any time that the professor takes more than two lectures to discuss any matter, it is almost guaranteed that she will ask you about it on a mid-term or final exam or both.

Just because a professor fails to ask a question about something, does not mean that you should refuse to tell her about it, but you had better be sure that she will agree with you that your answer is relevant.

Your history professor may give you an exam question such as:
Some modern historians believe that economic factors were the most important cause of the ... War. Other historians believe that political factors were the

most important causes. With which group do you most agree? Discuss your reasons in detail.

If there were only one correct answer, the professor would never have asked the question. You can choose either economic or political causes or both as long as you properly support your position. If, however, you are a little weak on the economic and political causes and loaded for bear on the geographical and social causes, your answer that the most important cause was neither economic or political because it was social or geographical will hold up well so long as you discuss the economic and political causes and state a good basis for your opinion.

Essay examination questions almost always ask you to compare, contrast, discuss, explain, define or choose. Read each question carefully, take a few moments to organize your thoughts and then reread the question. Be sure to include a thesis statement in the first paragraph so that the professor or her graduate assistant (the larger your class is the more likely that the professor will never see your examination paper) knows quickly where you are headed.

At the term break you can go back to your high school and thank your former English teachers who insisted on thesis statements when you saw no reasons for them.

How you answer the question is completely up to you, but be sure to answer the question, because every answer that fails to respond to the question is a wrong answer.

If the exam question were, "Fully discuss economic and political factors as causes of the ... War", then your answer can at most make passing reference to social and geographical factors. My experience as an attorney is that the most common mistake that witnesses make is not listening carefully to the question and then answering a question that wasn't asked.

Professors who stress concepts usually prefer essay exams. Professors who stress facts usually prefer multiple choice exams. A well designed exam differentiates among students based on their understanding of the course. No matter how difficult the test, the better prepared students will always score higher. An "easy" test is merely one that does not differentiate sufficiently between students with different levels of understanding. An "easy" test favors students who know less.

When I was in college, I taught life saving as a Red Cross Water Safety Instructor. My written exams were tough, but graded fairly. The highest score anybody ever got was a 94, but passing was about 50. I saw nothing to be gained by giving tests that measured my lack of work in preparing the test more than they measured what my students had learned. However, I was sure to tell my students in advance about the difficulty of my tests and my grading methods.

When Jonathan was in his first quarter of college, he told me that he was carrying a 75 quiz average in his economics class. I wasn't overly impressed by what at first glance seemed to be a "B-" or "C+". Jonathan then told me that in previous years a final average in the low 60's earned at least an A-. I didn't know his professor, but I did know that he knew how to discover what his students had learned.

On the other hand, I had a professor who intentionally gave easy quizzes and exams, which resulted in most students receiving high grades. He based his action on the theory that in the long run such positive reinforcement would encourage his students to learn more and retain more of what they learned. Do not waste your time looking for more professors like him, because he was a rare exception to the general rule.

XXVIII

ALL THE WORLD IS A STAGE

I have developed a Memorandum that I sometimes give to clients involved in litigation. Winning approval from a judge or jury is not altogether different from winning approval from a professor, so I am including here the full text. You may find some suggestions more relevant than others, but if you see no connections at all, you would do well to look again.

***

To:
From: Morris Seeskin
Re: Winning your lawsuit

With experience I have learned that conducting litigation is a lot like producing a theatrical production. You are more likely to receive rave reviews (win your case) if you carefully read and follow these guidelines.

    1. **PREPARE** by making your objective clear in your mind and reconsidering it from time to time. If you lose sight of your goal, in all likelihood we will fail together. The objective is to obtain a good result for you whether through trial or settlement. We are not trying to obtain revenge or teach the other side a lesson.

    2. **PREPARE** by always keeping in mind who your audience really is. You are playing to the judge and, if there will be one, to the jury and not to your opponent,

your friends and family, the press, or your attorney.

3. **PREPARE** by learning your lines. Only you can answer questions that are put to you. You must know what questions you will or might be asked and how you will answer. Learning your lines will be easier for you because your answers will be truthful.

4. **PREPARE** by learning everyone else's lines. You should know what your attorney will do and say, what opposing counsel and his client are likely to do and say, and what the judge and jury want to see and hear. Your opponent's version of the facts will be different than you might first think. Trust your attorney.

5. **PREPARE** by feeling. Your attorney will explain everything; your job is to do. Your attorney will talk about your pain and suffering; your job is to hurt. Your attorney will talk about your loss; your job is to lose again there in court.

6. **PREPARE** by reviewing the script. You must be completely in touch with every pleading filed in this case by you or another party. It is not enough for your attorney to be in touch with complaints, answers, replies, answers to interrogatories, documents produced, depositions, etc.; you must also know.

7. **PREPARE** your props. You and your attorney must know which documents

and objects you will or might need at trial and be sure that you are ready to produce them in court on cue.

    8.   **PREPARE** your costume. Review your costume (dress) with your attorney. How you look in court is most important.

    9.   **PREPARE** your calendar. Unless you and your attorney decide to the contrary, you must be an active participant in all stages of court proceedings. All other commitments take a back seat once litigation begins. **YES,** you must be in court for trial.

    10.   **REHEARSE** every act, every scene and every line over and over until you know the entire production.

    11.   **EVERY TIME YOU SAY ANYTHING, YOU LOSE GROUND!** Whether or not this is literally true, it is best to proceed as if it is. Be sure that everything you say and do works positively for you. Do not explain or elaborate unless both you and your attorney know what you intend to gain by doing so.

    12.   **WHEN YOU REACH THE POINT OF CLARIFICATION, STOP!** Answer every question fully but in the fewest words possible. Do not use a sentence if a word will do. Do not use a paragraph if a sentence will do. Do not use two paragraphs if one will do. Most witnesses talk too much, way too much. "Do you remember where you were on the evening of ...?" is a question calling for a "yes" or "no" answer and not a request for specific

information.

13. **LISTEN TO THE QUESTION!** There is a definite tendency for witnesses to answer questions they think were asked rather than the ones that were asked. What do you think the chances are of providing the correct answer to the question that actually was asked if you answer a different question that was not asked?

14. **DO NOT VOLUNTEER!** If no question is pending, remain silent. If a question is asked, answer it and then be quiet. The one and only one exception to this rule is that you may volunteer information that **with the full advance approval of your attorney** you both plan to get into the record **at a specific point in the proceedings**.

15. **THERE IS NO NEED TO TELL ALL THE TRUTH AT ONE TIME!** Completely apart from the fact that it is impossible to tell all the truth, the only thing that counts is the impact of your testimony and evidence on the trier of fact, the judge or the jury. If something needs to be made known, it will be, but only at the planned time.

16. **<u>NEVER</u> SURPRISE YOUR ATTORNEY IN PUBLIC!** Breaking this rule is the single best way to insure your loss in this case.

17. **IF YOU ARE UNCLEAR ON THE QUESTION, ASK FOR IT TO BE RESTATED OR REPHRASED!** An answer to a question you do

not fully understand almost always is incorrect.

18. **KNOW YOUR ENEMIES!** The other attorney is not on your side. HE IS YOUR ENEMY! Do not be taken in by his apparent reasonableness, costume, props, lines and generally friendly manner.

19. **KNOW YOUR OBJECTIVES!** If you lose sight of the first rule above, you will not get what you want. If you keep the correct focus, you may get what you want. There are no guarantees.

20. **TIMING IS IMPORTANT!** "WHEN" is at least as important as "WHAT".

21. **AN ATTORNEY WHO REPRESENTS HIMSELF HAS A FOOL FOR A CLIENT!** You may be the star of our production and even the major investor, but you have hired your attorney as script writer, producer, and director because you need help. Use his skills to your advantage.

22. **DO NOT ANTICIPATE THE NEXT QUESTION!** You have an attorney to anticipate the next question. Keep your focus on the present question and your answer to that question.

23. <u>**THINK!**</u>

24. **DO NOT GUESS!** If you are not sure about your answer, it is better to say so and to find out the answer later than it is to guess.

136

25. **YOU DO NOT HAVE TO KNOW EVERYTHING!** There is no rule that requires you to be an expert on everything. It is OK to defer to your attorney or other witnesses. BUT YOU HAD BETTER KNOW WHAT YOU NEED TO KNOW!

26. **IF IN DOUBT, KEEP QUIET!** It is most difficult to extract your foot from your mouth. Remembering later comes across better than unremembering.

27. **IGNORE YOUR FRIENDS!** Your family and friends do not have all the information necessary to evaluate your case and plan your strategy. They are well-meaning, but they are likely to mislead you.

28. **LISTEN TO YOUR ATTORNEY!** You are the client, but your attorney knows a lot more about winning in court than you do. If you do not believe this, why have you agreed to pay your good money for his legal services?

XXIX

THE ONLY THING IN LIFE THAT MAKES SENSE IS A HORSE RACE

When my father-in-law, Albert Fein, first told me that in life only horse races made sense, I laughed. Admittedly, a lot of what we call "life" does not seem to make sense at all. But horse races? As one who has spent only a few afternoons at the track, generally losing my $2.00 bets, horse races hardly seemed to make any sense at all, yet alone be the **only** thing that makes sense.

The more I thought about it, however, the more I came to see the wisdom in his observation. What makes sense about horse races is that the fastest horse in each race wins, assuming only an avoidance of bad luck. A horse cannot win based on how well it did in previous races. Neither can it win based on its perceived potential. Places are not awarded based on bloodlines, jockey skill, odds, or trainer competency. Races are simple. The fastest horse in each race wins.

Obviously, the same is true for people. The problem is that we don't often think about it that way. We think about upsets, when in fact there are only perceived favorites and underdogs. The better football team avoiding bad luck on a given day wins, no matter what the projections are.

138

While I was in college the nation's top ranked team came to Evanston as a huge favorite against Northwestern. The visitors won the coin flip and elected to receive. Coach Ara Parsegian had his team open the game with an on-side kick that was recovered. Northwestern promptly took it in for a touchdown. On the ensuing kick-off, the Wildcats kicked on-side again, recovered the ball again, and took it in for another touchdown. The visiting favorite never recovered. Was it an upset? Actually, the better coached team one that day.

The best students win, too. Grades in college are not based on class rank in high school or SAT scores. Good letters of recommendation are irrelevant in class. Grades aren't even based on your college GPA. Yes, you need to avoid bad luck. Being mildly sick on exam day may pull down your grade. It is better to be so sick as to cause you to miss the exam altogether in order that you can make it up later when you are well, than it is to be sick enough to affect your performance but not prevent you from taking the exam.

Years from now, when you look back on your college experience, the odds are that how you did will make sense. If you worked hard, you will be reaping the benefits. If not, you will be paying the price.

As a freshman at Northwestern I met Leon Wright, an African-American (then called "Black") football player from a small segregated high school in rural Georgia.

When compared with the education received by most other new students, he probably started college with a substantial handicap. (In horse race parlance he probably had a bad trainer and had only run against poor competition at bad tracks before running in the big time.)

From the start he was clear that he was at Northwestern because of his football skills, but that the key to his future lay in academic classrooms and not at Dyche Stadium. He had no illusions about a professional career. Actually, I don't think he ever played a down of varsity football. I was never in any of his classes.

Over the years I often wondered what happened to Leon Wright, whether he made anything of the opportunity provided by Northwestern. Then, in an institutional advertisement during an NCAA national basketball championship telecast, there was Leon Wright talking about how he had not been an athletic star, but that athletics had helped him get the education he needed to succeed in the business world. At my twenty-fifth college reunion I talked with him about the successful companies he now owns.

I really don't know Leon Wright at all, but I am sure that he worked his buns off in college in order to get a good start on the way to where he is today. My belief is that he is still working hard. His success is no accident; it makes sense.

140

XXX

DON'T DOUBT IT

If you are in doubt, do what is hard; in the long run it will be much easier. This is a basic truth of life that I needed about thirty-eight years to fully integrate. Although I learned it once, I still often forget it and need to be reminded again. When Aaron graduated from high school, I gave him an earlier draft of this book. Sometime later he pointed out that not only is the hard way easier in the long run, but also it is better.

I first heard this piece of wisdom from Dr. Ray Robertson. For a long time I chose not to believe him. As I observed the course of my own therapy and the progress or lack of progress of others in my group, I came to understand how very correct he was.

When I first accepted the notion that in the long run doing things the hard way would be easier than the path of least resistance, I was inclined to give Ray total credit for discovering and revealing to me this important truth. Without taking anything away from him, in recent years I have come to see that not just Ray Robertson, but each of the great teachers with whom I have studied, believed and taught the same principal, although each of them expressed it in different words.

If there was more than one way to solve a

plane geometry problem (and there always was), Seth Boyd refused to permit me to use the easier solutions until I could demonstrate that I had fully mastered the more difficult. When hand-held battery operated calculators first became popular, one of the metropolitan newspapers ran a feature story about Seth Boyd and his refusal to allow his students to use calculators in class. He insisted that each of his students demonstrate that he could think for himself before he would allow that student to use any short cuts.

Arthur Levin knew that I was not going to succeed at anything in or out of school if I chose to get along by doing the minimum. Apart from his regular teaching duties and advising the school newspaper, he invited selected students to his home one evening every week for a supplemental literature course. We read and discussed books that he believed his students should read in high school, but which had been omitted from the official school curriculum. As a journalism instructor and school newspaper advisor he set the standards for hard work that resulted in what was at the time probably the most consistently excellent high school newspaper in the country. Not only did I learn to write from him, but also I learned to be a critical reader.

Victor Rosenblum and Paul Schilpp never relented in asking students tough questions. No matter what the answer, they always were ready with more and more difficult questions. They insisted that each student master the educational process and think for himself. The mere parroting back of what others had written or said, even what they themselves had taught, was never enough.

Whenever I attempted to ease my way through or around a problem, Ray Robertson always forced me to deal head on with the matter at hand. Until I had the good fortune to be introduced to Ray, I did not appreciate the full value of confronting others, and I had no sense at all of the necessity of confronting myself on other than an intellectual level.

If you forget everything else in this book, you will still do well if you find a great teacher and listen carefully to what she is saying. That great teacher will not show you the path you seek, but she will help you to find your path. One way or the other, she will be giving you the same message as all the other great teachers: **If you are in doubt, do what is hard; in the long run it will be much easier.**

Made in the USA
Middletown, DE
12 February 2021